How to Blog for Profit
Without Selling Your Soul

New York Times Bestselling Author
Ruth Soukup

LIFE WELL LIVED PUBLICATIONS

This title is also available as an audiobook.
Visit eliteblogacademy.com/htbfp

Requests for information should be addressed to:

Ruth Soukup Omnimedia
307 Taylor Street
Punta Gorda, FL 33950

ISBN: 0692236511

ISBN 13: 9780692236512

Any internet addresses in this book are offered as a resource. They are not intended in any way to be an endorsement by Ruth Soukup or Life Well Lived Publications, nor does Ruth Soukup or Life Well Lived Publications vouch for the content of these sites for the life of this book.

Cover Design: Emma Beckett
Interior Design: Heather Moritz

First Edition, August 2013
Second Edition, July 2014
Third Edition, January 2020

ACCESS OUR FREE TRAINING

READ THIS FIRST

Studies show the best way to retain new information is to consume it in a variety of formats, and to apply what you are learning as you are learning it.

As a thank you for buying the written version of this book, I'd like to give you access to our free Easy Guide to Setting up Your Website, which will walk you through a step-by-step process of setting up your home base website on either WordPress, Shopify, or Squarespace.

TO DOWNLOAD IT, GO TO:

eliteblogacademy.com/homebase

ELITE BLOG
ACADEMY®

REFINE. GROW. MONETIZE. BUILD.

NOW IT'S YOUR TURN

Starting or growing an online business can often feel like a daunting process. There's so much information out there that it is hard to know exactly who to listen to, not to mention knowing what to focus on first.

At Elite Blog Academy®, we know for a fact that it's not just what action you take, but the order in which you do it in that makes the biggest difference for building a successful online business.

Our proven process and detailed, step-by-step instructions will get you moving faster, while our incredible community and support will set you up on the road for online business success in a way that's very hard to do all on your own.

Public enrollment to EBA only opens once a year, but you can watch our free training series now and say YES to starting your online business on the right track:

eliteblogacademy.com/training

How to Blog for Profit
Without Selling Your Soul

Table of Contents

introduction

Do You Have What It Takes?

"Do people actually still read blogs?"

It's a question I've been asked more times than I can count over the past few years, and one my friend Laura asked me recently. And while she might have been a tad blunt, I knew my friend Laura wasn't trying to put me down—even though this was, after all, my chosen career path.

What Laura really wanted to know—what everyone wants to know—is whether blogging is still relevant, and whether the time and effort it takes to make a blog successful is actually a worthwhile investment.

And it's a completely legitimate question.

Because maybe you've seen those headlines, the ones that declare, under no uncertain terms, that blogging is "over" and soon-to-be completely obsolete.

Believe me, I've seen them too.

In fact, I've been seeing those very same headlines every year since I first started blogging, way back in 2010 (also known as the Dark Ages of the internet!). Every few months, even back then, I'd read about how blogging is about to die, and how Facebook or Pinterest or Google algorithms are finally going to be the end of this industry, or that people's attention spans keep getting shorter and soon no one will have any patience for reading anything at all.

The sky is always falling, and bloggers better take cover.

But here's the deal, friend. Those headlines are wrong.

And after nearly ten years of blogging and six years of coaching more than 11,000 students in 60 countries worldwide to grow their own successful, profitable online businesses through Elite Blog Academy, I can tell you with complete confidence, that blogging is definitely NOT dead!

Not just that, I'd actually dare assert just the opposite—that there has never been a better time to harness the power of content marketing to start or grow a successful, profitable, and sustainable online business. One that allows you the freedom to craft the life you want, one that allows you to authentically connect with your customers, and one that makes money while you sleep.

For example, when Rosemarie Groner first decided to start an online business, she was a stay-at-home mom who spent her days running a small daycare from her home plus working two other part-time jobs on the side, just to make ends meet.

When she found Elite Blog Academy, she knew the comprehensive framework it provided was exactly what she needed to get on track, but it felt like a huge investment, one she wasn't even sure they could really afford, given their precarious financial situation. But, at her husband's encouragement, she resolved to take the class seriously and to do every single assignment in order, not moving ahead until each one was completed. She started in phase one, with refining her message, and in the process, she determined with crystal clarity that her mission was to provide financial advice for people who were overwhelmed with life, and who struggle with time management.

From there she moved to step two and began growing her audience, and then, as her traffic started to take off, she was ready to transition into phase three and begin focusing on monetization. When she moved into phase four, building her business, she felt equipped to build upon this framework of success she has created for herself.

When she first joined EBA, she was making just $18/month from her online business, but within a year she had grown her revenue to more than $30,000 a month. Most importantly, her life is completely different. Before Elite Blog Academy, she was running a daycare of 4 kids, had 2 additional side hustles, and worked on the blog at night. But now she works 20 hours a week, has financial freedom and a thriving business.

Likewise, when the travel guide industry she was in began tanking, Jennifer Maker knew she had two options. She could either get a new, good-paying job outside the home, or she could find other, better work to do at home. After some major soul searching, she realized she loved writing and sharing information, so she thought blogging would be a perfect fit.

For the first few months, Jennifer poured herself into blogging and gradually narrowed her focus from "all things mom related" to specifically DIY projects and crafts. She researched ways to monetize, how to improve, and how to expand her reach. And, while her traffic was growing, she just wasn't bringing in any money. Her best month brought in only $108. So she dug deeper, and she soon discovered Elite Blog Academy. Even though she put her tuition on a credit card because she was dead broke, she was determined to make it work.

And she did.

One year after starting EBA®, Jennifer's business was earning upwards of $20,000 a month, and within two years that number has skyrocketed to more than $100,000 a month. Her traffic has grown from 10,000 page views to more than 500,000 page views a month, and she has added more than 100,000 subscribers to her email list.

She's launched her own products, become an industry expert, and created a business she loves, one that she knows will continue to grow.

Blogging is far from dead.

And whether you are just looking to start a business and don't even know where to begin, or whether you've already got a product you want to sell, I believe there is no better time like the present to tap into the power of blogging and content marketing to grow your business.

BLOGGING DEFINED

Of course, before we go any further down this path, we should probably define what "to blog" actually means—at least as far as this book is concerned.

---

blog /bläg/

verb

to produce & publish any form of content online for the sake of establishing credibility, building rapport, and expanding your customer base; also sometimes called content marketing. Can include written blog posts, videos, podcasts, social media, and email.

And so, if your only point of reference for blogging goes back to that rambling travel diary your cousin Gwendolyn started on Blogspot back in 2006, then it is time to level up your understanding of what we're dealing with here.

Blogging, in the context that we will be discussing in this book, is a powerful tool for marketing whatever it is you have to sell, or whatever it is that you will end up selling. It is the vehicle you will use to grow your audience and establish a loyal tribe of raving fans, knowing that when you can build a customer base of people who know, like and trust you, then selling to them is the easy part.

Thus, when we talk about "blogging," we are talking about content marketing in the broad sense. It could mean posting written content on a blog, hosting a podcast, hosting a YouTube channel, or connecting with your audience via email. It's really all the same thing, just delivered differently.

WHAT ARE YOU SELLING?

But before we go any further, let's also just quickly address the "selling" part, because I know just the idea of selling something is what freaks a lot of people out. In fact, I can't even tell you how many EBA students have come to me over the years and said things like, "Ruth, I don't want to sell anything. I just want to have a little side business that makes money. Can't I just do that?"

And my answer is always a resounding "NO, you can't!"

So let's just get something clear from the get-go: if you want to have a business, you MUST sell something, because that is what a business does. Whether you are selling goods or services, intellectual property, or advertising space on your website, you are exchanging something of value that you have, for someone else's money. You can't have a business without the exchange of money, and you won't get any money without selling something.

It stands to reason, then, that it is also in your best interest to get good at selling, because the more you can sell, the more money you can make, and the more successful your online business will be.

And if that has left you with visions of needing to become some sort of sleazy used car salesman in order to make your business successful, then rest assured that this book is called "How to Blog for Profit Without Selling Your Soul" for a reason.

13

Because that's not what I want for you, nor is it how I've built my own 7-figure business. Instead, in this book, I'm going to teach you a whole different business model. It's the exact same framework that I teach in Elite Blog Academy, and it is designed to help you create a business built on trust, authenticity, and on serving your audience, not misleading them.

I call it the Upside-Down Business Model, and I'm not kidding when I tell you that it pretty much changes everything.

TURN YOUR BUSINESS UPSIDE DOWN

Of course, to understand what makes this new business model so powerful, you have to first understand how the traditional model for starting a business has always worked. In a traditional business model, you create a product or service. You then open a store, or a restaurant, and then you work really hard to try to find customers to buy your product or service, shop in your store, or eat at your restaurant.

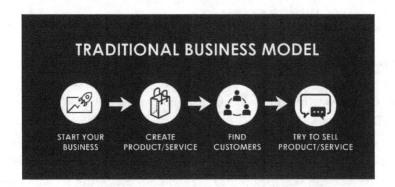

If you've ever owned a traditional small business or grew up in a family that owned one, you know how tough it can be to make it work. It is a life of endless hustle, of taking big risks, making big investments and taking out big loans in hopes that those risks will pay off, and you will eventually be able to get your feet on solid ground. And, as the statistics tell us, many of those businesses never do. 20% of all small businesses fail in their first year, 50% of all small businesses will fail by year five, and only 33% of small businesses will make it to year 10[1].

Pretty scary right?

But it is also interesting to pay attention to WHY most small businesses fail. Because as it turns out, 82% of small businesses fail because of cash flow problems. They simply don't have enough capital to keep going or to get their feet off the ground.

Phil Knight, in his riveting autobiography, *Shoe Dog*, which tells his story of founding Nike and getting the company off the ground, speaks directly of this struggle. In fact, one of the most interesting aspects of his story is just how much his company struggled with cash flow—for more than 20 years! Even when they were doing millions and millions of dollars in sales and securing the biggest celebrity endorsements, they constantly fought to make ends meet. It wasn't until they finally went public in the 1980s, after struggling for nearly 25 years, that their cash flow issue finally went away.

Money makes the world go 'round, and when it comes to starting a small business, a lack of cash will break you.

But it is not just the lack of cash that leads to doom. You see, despite their cash issues, Nike survived because they had an amazing product, one that the market was desperate for.

Unfortunately, that is not always the case. Believe it or not, when asked WHY their business failed, more than half of the failed business owners cited the fact that there was either no market need for their product, they chose the wrong product altogether, or they didn't listen to their customers.

If you look at all that data, it is pretty clear that far and away the two biggest reasons most small businesses fail is either a.) a lack of cash to keep things running or b.) a lack of felt need—meaning a solution that people are actually looking for, for the product they are selling.

But the beauty of content marketing and starting an online business is that it essentially avoids those two problems altogether. The framework we teach at Elite Blog Academy—and the framework I will be following here in this book—flips that traditional business model upside down, and in the process, makes it better.

THE UPSIDE DOWN BUSINESS MODEL™

REFINE
YOUR MESSAGE

GROW
YOUR AUDIENCE

MONETIZE
YOUR PLATFORM

BUILD
YOUR BUSINESS

You see, we don't start with a product that the market may or may not want, and then hope we can find customers to buy it. We don't pour thousands of dollars into research and development, opening a brick and mortar location, or hiring a bunch of people we might need.

Instead, we start by developing a relationship with our readers and customers. We work first to refine our message, to figure out exactly who we are talking to, what their felt needs are, and what we want to say. And while this does take an investment of time, it doesn't take a lot of cash. In fact, it's almost risk-free, because if your message isn't resonating, you can change it, hone it, and refine it until it does.

And then, once we've got that down, we begin expanding our reach and growing our audience, all while continuing to refine our message, develop trust, and an authentic relationship. And once again, the risk here is minimal. It takes time, but not a ton of cash.

It is only then that we start adding in the monetization piece, but by this point, it becomes easy. We understand our market. We've established trust and a real relationship. We know what our audience is already asking for, and now we can give it to them. When we create products, we don't have to go out looking for customers because we already have them.

And from there, we build our business. We now have something we didn't have before—capital—and so we go back through the cycle and can take slightly bigger risks as we continue to refine, grow, and monetize. We start looking at our blog as an asset of our business, and we figure out how to create sustainable, long term growth.

It's a business model that works, and best of all, it is one that works without all the pitfalls that cause most small business models to fail.

If you have the grit to put in the work on the front end, to put in the initial investment of time and energy, and to keep going and not quit, you will eventually reap the rewards.

And that's pretty amazing.

WHO THIS BOOK IS FOR

Which I suppose leads me back to the question I started with—do you have what it takes? Do you have what it takes to build a successful online business? Do you have what it takes to leverage the power of content marketing in order to cultivate a tribe of raving fans and loyal customers? Do you have what it takes to turn your preconceived notions of what a business is supposed to look like upside down and pioneer a whole new path?

Since you're still reading, I'm going to guess yes.

But I'm also going to guess that the question you really want to know the answer to is this: Will this book help ME? Is this the right book for *my* business, *my* dream, *my* situation? Is it really worth my time to keep reading?

So here's who this book is actually for:

> → You don't yet have a blog or an online business, but you are thinking about starting one. You want to have a better understanding of exactly

what it takes to be successful, and what you'll need to do to get started.

→ You've already started your blog or online business, but it's been a struggle and right now you just feel stuck. You're pretty sure you might be missing something. You're constantly distracted by all the things "everyone" is telling you to do, not to mention confused by the seemingly contradictory advice, and you just want a clear path to follow.

→ You're not that interested in writing a blog, but you've started (or would like to start) a podcast or a YouTube channel, and you want to know how to monetize in order to turn it into a successful online business.

→ You already have an established business, store, or product, and you want to know how to use content marketing to get more customers.

→ You are an author, or an aspiring author, who wants to sell more books or land a book deal with a publisher, and who has been told that in order to do either of those things you need to have a platform.

As you can see, the business model I'm going to teach you in this book—the same business model I've used to grow my own 7-figure business, and that I've taught since 2014 at Elite Blog Academy—is a business model that works for a variety of circumstances and situations.

It doesn't matter whether you are just getting started, or whether you've been at this for a while; nor does it matter whether your ultimate goal is to write a book, sell products, or find more customers for your brick and mortar store. And it certainly doesn't matter if your content takes the form of writing or video or audio or photos on social media.

The overarching strategy is all about building a tribe of raving fans who know, like, and trust you; because when you have that, everything else falls into place.

Of course, there are a few people who this book won't be right for. I wouldn't recommend it for anyone who's not willing to take action or to actually apply what you are learning. Nor would I recommend it for anyone who is looking for a get-rich-quick scheme, or a way to make a million dollars by next week. And I most definitely wouldn't recommend this book if you think you already know everything there is to know about blogging.

If that's you, then it might just be time to put the book down and walk away. No hard feelings—I promise.

And if you're not sure? Then before you go any further, I recommend you take our free blogging assessment which will tell you whether you have what it takes to be a successful entrepreneur or online business owner. You can find it online at **assessment.eliteblogacademy.com**.

A FEW DISCLAIMERS

And then finally, before we dive into the nitty-gritty of what it takes to create a successful and profitable content marketing business, I want to issue a few disclaimers and qualifiers about myself, my expertise, and the topics I won't be covering, so that you can know exactly what to expect before you continue reading.

This is now the third edition of this book. I wrote the first edition of *How to Blog for Profit (Without Selling Your Soul)* in 2013, shortly after my husband Chuck had quit his job to be a stay-at-home dad, so that I could focus full-time on turning my blog into a legitimate—and sustainable—online business.

I published the expanded 2nd edition a year later, and that edition went on to become my best selling book of all time- selling close to a half-million copies over the past five years.

My business has grown a lot since 2014, from a low 6-figure solo operation to a high 7-figure company with multiple divisions and a whole team of people to make it run. As such, much of my business strategy has necessarily evolved as well.

Thus, my goal for this third edition of *How to Blog for Profit* is to expand on some of the most important things I've learned in the past few years about blog creation, traffic platform growth, monetization, and turning a blog into a thriving, profitable business.

Here are a few things you should know about me, and about what you can and can't expect to find in this book:

1. I started my business as a personal lifestyle blog called Living Well Spending Less, which covered a wide variety of topics, including food & recipes, home & life advice, and money-saving tips. It has since grown and evolved into a full-fledged online media company called Ruth Soukup Omnimedia, which focuses on four primary areas—Lifestyle, Business, Productivity, and Motivation. I've written six bestselling books, created a physical product called the Living Well Planner that we manufacture and ship all over the world, and now host a top-rated podcast called Do It Scared with Ruth Soukup. And while that is a lot of different things, which gives me a pretty broad understanding of the content marketing world, it is important to know that **my area of expertise is not all-inclusive, and it is possible that some of what I share in this book will not perfectly fit your own business or situation.**

2. My own business has generated a six-figure income from the monetization strategies discussed in this book since 2013, and has generated a healthy seven-figure income since 2015. What's more, since 2014 I have coached more than 11,000 Elite Blog Academy students in 60 countries worldwide, and in every niche imaginable, to build their own dream businesses. **My goal is not to help you create a business that looks exactly like mine, but to help you leverage the power of content marketing to grow your own successful, profitable, and sustainable online business.**

3. **This is not a technical guide for how to set up a blog or website.** If you are looking for a step-by-step, how-to manual on setting up a blog, or establishing accounts on social media, this is not it. That said, we do have

some wonderful resources available on our website at eliteblogacademy.com, including a free *Easy Tech Guide to Setting Up Your Website* that you can find at eliteblogacademy.com/homebase.

The purpose of *How to Blog for Profit* is to help you leverage the power of content marketing in your business, regardless of whether you've just begun or whether you've been in business for years. It is filled with practical takeaways and actionable steps to help you assess and create the most successful plan for your own audience. And regardless of what many online marketers will tell you, there is no one "right" way to make money online. My goal is to give you the tools to reach your own business goals, whether those goals be to start a business, grow your platform, make more money, sell your product, get more customers, or all of the above.

PHASE 1 | REFINE

Refining your message is all about figuring out who you are talking to, what you are going to say, how you are going to say it, and how you are going to present it. And while that sounds simple, for most content creators, this is the hardest (yet most essential) part of starting a successful online business. This is the foundation on which the rest of your business will be built, which means it is essential to get it right.

In this section of the book, you'll start with the fundamentals by looking at what it takes to get started with building your foundation for a profitable and successful online business, and answer the two most fundamental questions for your business. From there, you'll work on developing amazing content. You'll learn how to use an editorial calendar, how to brainstorm an endless stream of ideas, and how to create consistently excellent killer content. Finally, you'll also look at how to present that amazing content in a visual way that draws readers in and keeps them coming back for more.

chapter 1

How to Get Started

"Honey, that's the stupidest thing you've ever said."

It was the summer of 2010, and that was my husband Chuck's reaction the first time I excitedly told him my big idea—that I wanted to make enough money from my just-launched blog that he could quit his job.

He wasn't really trying to be mean, he was just being his regular honest self. And I couldn't really blame him. It did seem like a completely crazy idea. Make money from a blog? Who does that?

And yet, I knew there were people who were doing it. My two-week foray into blogging opened up a whole new world to me, and I somehow just knew that if other people could make money at it, then I could too.

Even if I had no idea what I was doing. Even if I was a stay-at-home mom of two toddlers, just trying to find something productive to do that didn't involve going to Target. Even if I still didn't understand HOW bloggers made money, or even how to get people to read my website.

The truth is that I started my blog out of little more than desperation. That summer Chuck and I had argued nonstop about my Target habit, and my spending that was quickly spiraling out-of-control. Stuck at home in a new town, with two young kids and no friends, I badly needed a new hobby that wasn't shopping.

After one big, make-it-or-break-it fight, I finally agreed to stick to a monthly budget, then started a blog called *Living Well Spending Less* to chronicle my journey.

Amazingly enough, it worked. I learned to save and use coupons and began journeying towards a simpler life (Of course, all that is a story for a different book[2]!).

This book is about blogging for profit, something I've also learned a lot about since I first began. In fact, within my first few weeks of blogging I realized two important things: First, I was *born* to do this job. After all, what other job would allow me to do all the things I love—cook, clean, craft, organize, and write—and still give me the flexibility to stay at home with my kids or to literally work from anywhere? Second, I realized I could *actually make money doing what I loved*. From that moment on, I set out to learn everything I possibly could about professional blogging.

So while my public journey was about learning to control my spending, my private journey was learning the behind-the-scenes business of creating a successful and profitable content marketing-based online business. And those two paths intertwined so tightly that I'm fairly sure I couldn't do one without the other.

That is exactly the way it should be.

Much of the time, content marketing—whether it be through blogging, podcasting, social media, or video—is incredibly personal. Your readers and followers don't just come to read what you have to write, they come for you; for your unique voice, perspective, style and ideas. You become someone that they can relate to, someone who feels like a friend, and someone in whom they are willing to invest emotional energy. You become someone that they know, like, and trust.

Thus, the real secret to successfully blogging for profit is learning how to be real and maintain authenticity with your audience, while at the same time successfully navigating the behind-the-scenes waters of running a business and building a brand. There will always be a balance that you have to strike, between your public persona and your business persona. You might even think of it as the difference between the onstage performance and everything that happens backstage to support the show.

And while that might seem hard, or even impossible, it's really, truly *not*.

Just stay you.

That's all you have to do. Learn from, but don't try to emulate other bloggers, influencers, and online business owners. Don't get so wrapped up in trying to build your stats that you try to be everything to everyone all at once, and forget to stay authentic to you. Don't get so obsessed with making money as fast as possible that you find yourself selling or promoting things you don't even like. Just stay you. That's it!

Easy, right?

EVERYONE STARTS AT ZERO

I'm going to give you a whole lot of advice in this jam-packed little book, and so many action items for your to-do list that at times you will feel like your head might actually explode. But if you were to take away only ONE piece of wisdom, it would be this:

> *We all start at zero.*

In a world where we are surrounded by influencers, bloggers, podcasters, YouTubers, and online business owners to compare ourselves to, this one essential truth is all too easy to forget—that every single person you see killing it online, every blogger you see who's somehow managed to gather a following or is making all kinds of money—they all started at zero.

Zero pageviews.
Zero downloads.
Zero followers.
Zero income.

Zero. Zip. Zilch. Nada. Nothing.

Yes, some bloggers and influencers do manage to grow their platform faster than others. But for most of us, it takes time. And regardless of where we end up, we all start at zero.

Jon Acuff puts it a different way when he says "don't compare your beginning to someone else's middle."

The first time I heard him say this at a blogging conference called *Blissdom* in 2012, I felt as though I had been physically slapped across the face. In that moment I realized that nearly all of my insecurities with blogging came from comparing myself to others and from feeling like everyone else was somehow doing it better than I was.

Feeling like I wasn't good enough and trying to emulate other people's success had paralyzed me. At the time I was operating four different blogs. I was making a little bit of money, but I was working nonstop and I was miserable. Truth be told, I was ready to quit.

In that moment, I made a decision that changed my life. I decided to stop comparing and to simply put my head down and get to work on the things that I actually cared about, not just the things that were earning an income.

Four months later I sold the two sites that were actually earning an income and completely shut down the third, not knowing whether I was throwing away any chance that I'd ever make enough money to support my family. I was disappointed, but at that point I knew I just needed to get refocused on my core message.

On my one remaining blog, the one I had started with, I decided to get clear about who I was writing to—my avatar—and to simply begin writing the things that I knew would resonate with her, without worrying about whether I was saying the "right" things, the "popular" things, or even the "profitable" things.

I gave myself permission to be authentic, to be real with my readers, and to be different than everyone else. For a while I even stopped reading other blogs because I found that when I did, all those insecurities would come creeping back in.

And then something amazing happened.

That same little neglected blog, the one I had all but abandoned as I chased what I thought was the way to "fast money," began to grow. Traffic grew slowly at first, and then faster and faster, until in less than six months' time it was more than ten times larger than what it had been. Those posts written with my avatar in mind actually resonated with the very people I was writing to. And while there certainly were some people who absolutely hated what I had to say, the ones who were my people knew they had found their place.

And guess what else? With an increase in traffic came an increase in income, and incredibly just eight months after I sold what I thought were my two "money-making" blogs, and almost giving up the dream of being a full-time professional blogger, my husband was finally able to walk away from the engineering job he hated to become a stay-at-home-dad.

We've never looked back.

That year, 2013, was my first 6-figure year as a blogger. 2015 was my first 7-figure year, and by 2018, my company had hit the $5 million mark. In hindsight, it all happened SO fast, but I can tell you that in the midst of all those early mistakes, it certainly didn't feel fast.

Just the opposite, in fact. Those first few years felt endless. It felt so hard. It felt so painful. It felt like I would never get there. It felt like I had no idea what I was doing (which I didn't), like everyone else was moving faster, and like I was possibly wasting hours of my time on a dream that was never going to come true.

And that's exactly why it is so important to remember that everyone starts at zero.

Because when you are in it, when you are just starting out, it feels like you must be doing something wrong. Progress is slow. You don't feel like you're getting anywhere. Everyone else seems like they've got it together, while you feel like you're falling behind. Your trajectory is completely flat, and every day you wonder if you've made a mistake, and whether you are ever going to get there.

But what I've learned from my own experience, and from the thousands of students I've taught at Elite Blog Academy, is that the trajectory for starting a successful on-line business looks something like this:

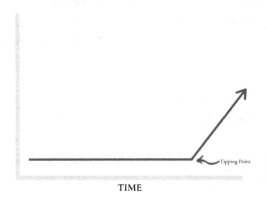

TIME

It's a very long, flat line followed by a steep incline.

And for some business owners, that long flat line takes 6 months. For others, that long flat line takes years. But it always feels endless, because when you are in it, you don't actually know how long it is going to take.

But then—and I have seen this happen over and over and over again—you finally hit the tipping point. The magic moment where something finally clicks, something finally connects, and suddenly both your traffic and your income take off.

And here's what else I know. The trajectory I illustrated *will* happen - if you're willing to do the work, to keep going, and keep trying until you finally figure out what works. But know that it could take a while. Maybe even years.

For me, it took from 2010 until 2013. Three very long years.

Which begs the question, are you willing to work at this for as long as it takes—maybe even three full years—without ever knowing whether your efforts will actually pay off?

I hope so.

I don't want to sugarcoat this: starting a business, whether it's online or not, is *hard*. It takes grit and perseverance, a willingness to make mistakes, to take risks, and to keep going no matter what.

My own lessons in blogging and starting an online business were hard-fought, but they taught me a lot. My goal for this book is to shorten your learning curve and to hopefully help you not make some of the mistakes that I did, or the ones I've seen my students make over the past five years.

But ultimately the biggest indicator of your success will be your willingness to stick with it, and your refusal to quit.

We all have to start at zero, and we all have to figure out what works for our own unique message and for our unique audience. Your journey will probably not look like mine, and it probably won't look exactly like anyone else's either. If you are constantly comparing yourself to people who are farther down their path, you will defeat yourself before you even begin. And if you give yourself permission to give up, you'll never actually give yourself a chance to succeed.

So right here, right now, before we go any further, I want you to commit to keep going, to keep trying, and to keep figuring it out. Because, as Marie Forleo often points out, "everything is figureoutable."

And then, just be YOU. Accept where you are in this moment, then own your journey and open yourself up to the possibility of learning everything you can along the way.

FIRST THINGS FIRST

I already know that for some of you, your temptation with this book will be to skip to the "good" stuff—the chapters all about how to make money. But I'm going to ask you to try not to do that, or at the very least, skim it over and then come back to the beginning. Building a strong foundation on which to build your online business is incredibly important. In fact, it's absolutely essential. For now, you'll just have to trust me on that.

The thing is, if your only goal in starting a blog or an online business is to make money, content marketing might not be the right fit for you.

I know what you're thinking. *But the title of this book is* How to Blog for Profit! *Why else would I have bought it if my goal wasn't to make money?!*

So let me rephrase:

If your ONLY goal in starting a blog or an online business is to make money, you will fail.

There are far easier and much surer and faster ways to earn money right away than by starting a content marketing-based business. You could get a part-time or full-time job, become a freelance consultant or writer, a virtual assistant, or a window washer or house cleaner, or start selling your stuff on Ebay, Craigslist, or Facebook. All of those things would put cash in your pocket quickly, though not all of them would be sustainable, and not all of them would give you the potential for long-term, sustainable passive income.

When you decide to start a content marketing-based business, you are choosing to play the long game. You're choosing to front-load your time and effort, knowing that the payoff will come later. Sometimes much later.

Now please know this is not meant to dissuade you from starting a blog. I love blogging! Remember my two revelations? The first was that I was born to do this. No other job could allow me to pursue all the things I am passionate about and still give me the flexibility to stay home with my kids, take a month-long road trip, start working at five in the morning so that I can be done by noon, or allow me to travel and cook, craft, and write, and still call it *work*.

It is also not meant to dissuade you from trying to make money with your blog. Anyone who starts a blog or an online business can and should be able to profit from that effort. But the effort—lots of it—comes first, long before you ever make a penny. Also, if you are not excited and passionate about what you are writing, about the audience you are serving, and if you don't love and care about what you do, the money will never be great enough to justify all the sacrifices, all the time spent, all the struggles and frustrations, and heartache along the way.

The place to start, if you want to (eventually) blog for profit, is with great, amazing, compelling, bring-me-back-for-more **content**. In other words, your blog or podcast or YouTube channel has to be awesome. *You* have to be awesome. And that sounds harder than it is, because chances are, *you are already awesome* in some way.

So find *your awesome* and create your business around *that*.

What do you love more than anything? Who are you most passionate about helping or serving? What kind of activities make you want to jump out of bed in the morning, or what gets you fired up to a point that you just can't stop talking about it? What is it that you are really good at? What do others ask you about? What topics are you naturally drawn to? What subject do you love to read about?

If you already have a blog and you've been creating content about something else, something other than what you are truly passionate about, it is time to make a few changes. Never be afraid to steer your content in a new direction, if that is where your heart is telling you to go. More than anything else, your readers crave authenticity; if you are holding back, they will sense it. Give them everything you've got. Make it awesome.

And before you psych yourself out by thinking that there is too much competition, or too many people already out there doing what you want to do, let me just tell you that there is a whole lot of room for awesome in the blogosphere. Don't think that because other people are already awesome, you can't be awesome too. Blogging is not a zero-sum game. We live in a world of abundance, not scarcity, and there will never be enough awesome, because there is already so much out there that ISN'T. People *crave* awesome. And there is nothing stopping you from being awesome.

So start there.

SET UP YOUR HOME BASE

For most people, getting started will mean choosing a name and a URL, then setting up a website. Because if you are going to start a content-marketing based business—whether it be a blog, podcast, or a YouTube channel—you are going to need a home base—a place where people, soon *your* people, can find you. A place that draws people in and lets them know, at a glance, what you and your business are all about, and what they can expect to gain from being there.

And can I just be totally honest with you?

For some reason, this very first step, this set-up part, tends to be the part of the process that freaks people out the most. Maybe it's that it feels too technical. Maybe it's that you're afraid of making a mistake, or getting it wrong, or having it not be perfect. Maybe it's that actually setting up a real live website, with a real live URL will mean that you're actually committing to this idea. Or maybe it's just that the first step is always the hardest step.

But whatever the reason, the only real solution is to just rip off the proverbial band-aid, take a deep breath, and DO IT SCARED!

So pay attention, because this part is important: You cannot let the technical aspect of setting up a website intimidate you, nor do I want you to let your confusion or inexperience be the thing that keeps you from getting started.

Remember what I said a minute ago about everyone having to start at zero? That goes for the tech stuff too. Every blogger or online business owner has, at some point, had to struggle through trying to figure out how to do something on their blog or website. Whether it be the initial setup, installing a plugin or some HTML code for a sidebar widget, publishing their first post or setting up their navigation bar, they started from zero.

Know from the get-go that there is going to be a learning curve if you have never set up a website before. There will be lots of things that you have to either try to figure out yourself—because that's what Google is for—or that you have to hire someone more technical than you to help you with.

That said, I guarantee that most of your tech issues are in your head more than anything else. What's really holding you back isn't actually the tech stuff, but the fear and belief that you won't be able to figure it out.

Because these days the tools that are available to help you set up your website are incredibly user-friendly! Many were designed specifically for people who aren't good at tech. They're so straightforward and easy to use that you don't have to be a computer programmer or a graphic designer to put together a beautiful, professional-looking website.

Here is a brief breakdown of my recommended tools and options for getting your website up and running. For a much more in-depth analysis, step-by-step instructions, links to exclusive setup offers for EBA readers, and all the most up-to-date information on website options, visit eliteblogacademy.com/homebase.

OPTION 1: WORDPRESS

Overview: WordPress[3] is, more-or-less, the industry standard for website platforms. Overall, it offers the most flexibility for both design and functionality, and is why it's our primary recommendation to all of our students at Elite Blog Academy. WordPress itself is free, but you will have to pay a third party for hosting. (See eliteblogacademy.com/homebase for hosting recommendations and setup instructions.)

Pros: Inexpensive; endless options for customization; lots of prebuilt themes to choose from; thousands of available plugins (both free and paid) that allow for additional functionality; good for SEO; specific themes available for podcasters and/or YouTubers.

Cons: Not an all-in-one option; requires slightly more technical prowess than either Squarespace or Shopify.

Best for: Anyone who feels comfortable enough with the technology to figure things out themselves; anyone who wants the ability to fully customize their design; podcasters.

OPTION 2: SQUARESPACE

Overview: SquareSpace is a sleek and user-friendly all-in-one option for building and hosting your website. It will walk you through the process of selecting a template, then allow you to somewhat customize your template with your own colors and photos.

Pros: Easy to use; beautiful templates; all-in-one option for domain, hosting, and design allows you to get up and running very quickly; includes options for eCommerce.

Cons: More expensive than WordPress; not fully customizable; most templates are for setting up websites, not blogs; and not a great setup for podcasts.

Best for: Beginners; anyone who feels easily intimidated by tech; anyone who wants to get up and running as quickly as possible, and doesn't want to be overwhelmed by options.

OPTION 3: SHOPIFY

Overview: Shopify is an easy-to-use eCommerce platform that offers thousands of different themes and is designed first and foremost to help you sell your products and manage your inventory. Most themes include the ability to add a blog.

Pros: Easy to use; lots of beautiful themes to choose from; designed to showcase and sell your products (both physical and digital); eCommerce options already built-in.

Cons: Expensive; more focused on eCommerce than blogging; additional paid apps & plugins used to add functionality can add up costs quickly.

Best for: Someone who already has an inventory of products to sell.

Regardless of which platform or tool you decide to use to host your website, you will first need to choose a name for your business, as well as find an available URL. This can sometimes be a challenging process, as many times your first choice of name and domain name may not be available.

That's why I believe it is best to not overthink the naming process. Yes, you want a great name that is easy to remember, that fits what you want to do, and that you love, but it doesn't need to be perfect, and chances are good that it won't be your first choice. Just know that up front.

So here's how to approach it.

First, set the timer for 15 or 20 minutes and brainstorm a bunch of different possibilities—as many names as you can possibly think of. Just start writing without self-editing or overthinking. Think about what you're passionate about, the genre you want to blog in, or something unique about you or your life, and get as many names onto that piece of paper as you possibly can.

Your next step then, once you've brainstormed a whole list of names, is to begin vetting the names and phrases to see which ones might actually work. To do that, check to make sure the name you have in mind is actually available as a URL—which means checking Bluehost.com, GoDaddy.com, or another domain buying service to make sure the domain name isn't already reserved. You'll also want to check social media channels to see if that name is already out there, since you'll want your name and your social media handles to match, or at least be pretty similar in order to avoid confusion.

While you're researching, also do a Google search to find out if any other blog, business, or product has the same name. Then go to https://www.uspto.gov/ to do a trademark search and find out whether a trademark has been filed for that name in a similar industry. (Trust me, the last thing you want to do is launch a blog that will compete in search engines with another product or business!)

If you're having trouble finding an available name you like, you may also want to consider making up a word that fits what you want to talk about (like the person who coined the term "mompreneur," for example).

Your final step, then, is to pick the best name that's available. Again, it might not be the perfect name, but that's okay. Remember that **the name of your blog will not make or break your success**. So try to take the pressure off yourself, and just make a decision so that you can move on. What's really most important at this stage is to just get it up and going. You can even change the name later!

GET CLEAR ABOUT WHAT YOU DO & WHO YOU SERVE

Believe it or not, choosing a name for your business is not actually the most important piece of getting started. The reality is that everything on the Internet is editable, which means that if you choose the wrong name today, you can always change it later.

It is actually far more important that you start out with clarity on what it is that you actually want to accomplish with your business. And so, before you get your heart set on a particular name (or before you get yourself all stressed out about selecting the perfect name), you'll need to be able to answer two essential questions about your business.

> 1.) What will you talk about?
> 2.) Who will you be talking to?

So let's take them one at a time, shall we?

First, what do you want to talk about? What is it that you will actually write about, day after day after day? What will be the topic or subject matter that you become known for? What are the interests that will bring people to you?

The whole point of content marketing, whether it be on a blog, podcast, or YouTube channel, is to use content around a particular topic as a way of drawing people—your potential customers—into your orbit, and to get them to know, like, and trust you.

And that starts with knowing what particular topic your content is actually going to be about.

So ask yourself the following questions again:

• What do you love more than anything?

- What are you most passionate about?
- What makes you want to jump out of bed in the morning, or gets you fired up to a point that you just can't stop talking about it?
- What is it that you are really good at?
- What do others ask you about?
- What topics are you naturally drawn to?
- What subject do you love to read about?
- What do you wish you were better at, or are you actively working on improving in your own life?
- What are your hobbies or interests?
- What is something you think you could help people with?

Awesome comes from your own passion and energy about a topic. Because if you don't care about what you have to say, why would anyone else?

That said, it is important to understand that not every topic you are passionate about will be the basis for a successful, profitable blog or online business. So as you are thinking about what you are most passionate about, also be thinking about which of those ideas and topics might also be the most marketable or the most interesting to other people.

Contrary to popular belief, there is not just one "type" of blog or niche that does well, or that has strong potential for monetization. On the contrary, I've seen my students at Elite Blog Academy earn a full-time living from a huge variety of niches, from the very broad to the very focused.

These include:
- Health & fitness
- Food & recipes
- Marriage & relationships
- Pets & animals
- Natural living & homesteading
- Faith & religion
- Fashion & lifestyle

- Travel
- Business & entrepreneurship; including everything from getting your dream job to being a working mom, to starting your own business.
- Personal growth & motivation; including self-help, productivity, and goal setting.
- Home & decor; including everything from cleaning & organizing to interior design, to DIY.
- Parenting; including everything from handling a difficult pregnancy to getting your baby to sleep, disciplining your toddlers, to resources for school-aged kids to raising teenagers that you like (and many, many more).
- Crafting; including sewing, knitting, crocheting, paper crafts, and more.
- Super niche topics; including a blog devoted to the care and love of succulents, a blog about monarch butterflies, and a blog about female hair loss—just to name a few.

And while knowing WHAT you want to talk about is both important and essential, it is not *quite* enough. Because you also need to know WHO you will be creating this content for.

Which, of course, brings us to the second question—who will you be talking to? And by that I don't just mean what type of people you will be writing to, ie. some general demographic such as "middle-class urban women ages 35-50."

Instead, I mean *who is your avatar?* The one single person that represents your ideal customer; the one and only person you will be thinking of every time you create a piece of content.

When it comes to creating a successful, profitable blog, there is nothing more important than understanding exactly who you are writing to.

Because here's the little-known secret that so many content marketers miss: The most successful businesses are the ones that actively seek to help their readers and customers. They are the ones that provide practical solutions to their problems, encouragement for their doubts, fears, and struggles, or inspiration for when they are feeling low or instruction for when they want to learn how to do something. The most successful online businesses—even when written from a personal point of view—make it about the reader.

And that means, before you do anything else, you need to know who your audience is…what drives them, what scares them, what they want most, their deepest struggles and frustrations, and how they think. Your audience needs to be REAL to you.

That's where a customer avatar comes in.

And if you don't know who your avatar is, then before you go any further, you need to figure this out and actually get clear about exactly who it is you will be serving.

You can't write to everyone, nor do you want to. Because when you are writing to everyone, you are really writing to no one.

At the very least, you should be able to answer the following questions about your avatar or ideal customer:

- What does his or her basic demographics look like? What is his or her gender, age, marital status, income level, occupation, etc.?
- What are his or her hobbies?
- Where does he or she shop?
- What does your avatar read? What are his or her favorite books and magazines?
- What blogs or websites does your avatar visit on a regular basis? What podcasts does he or she listen to?
- What religion does your avatar practice? How devout is he or she?
- What political beliefs does your avatar hold?
- What are your avatar's spending habits?
- What keeps your avatar up at night? What is his or her deepest fear?
- What subjects or issues does your avatar avoid facing?
- What are your avatar's greatest opportunities?

- What are your avatar's hopes and dreams? Who or what do they aspire to be?
- What does your avatar hope to accomplish in the next year?
- What does your avatar value?
- What is your avatar struggling with right now? What are they hiding from others?

Once you've taken the time to answer these questions and have a clearer sense of the person you are writing to, I recommend taking it one step further and actually working to make him or her completely real to you. Give your avatar a name. Find a photo that represents them. Write down their story, and re-read it every single day, until writing to your avatar feels like you are writing to a friend.

EBA Case Study:
Shelley Jefsen, *Mama Duck*

Shelley originally started blogging in 2009, but it wasn't until 2018 that she decided to get serious and join Elite Blog Academy. As it turns out, that one simple decision would lead to some of her biggest breakthroughs.

Shelley has always known that her perspective on parenting was a little bit different, but she wasn't sure how to convey that message, or even how to attract the right people—the mamas, like her, that knew there was a better way to parent than just throwing up your hands and giving up.

And so, while most bloggers and online business owners focused on increasing their traffic as fast as possible, Shelley quickly realized that she needed to first build a strong foundation. And so, before she worked on traffic, she first focused on refining her voice and identifying her avatar to ensure her content would resonate with the right audience.

This was incredibly powerful, because she felt like she had been given permission to be herself. She finally embraced the idea that it was okay to speak only to the person that wanted to hear from her, even if she couldn't see them yet.

And you know what? She didn't have to chase anyone because they found her. And as a result, her business, filled with her own tribe of loyal raving fans, continues to grow exponentially.

SET UP YOUR STRUCTURE

Once you've landed on a name, set up your home base, and created clarity by answering those two most essential questions about your business—what will you talk about, and who will you be writing to—the final step is to build yourself a structure and develop a clear plan for how you'll organize the content on your site.

Research has shown that you've only got a few seconds to capture a new reader's attention before they get bored and move on. There are lots of different things you can do to try to grab their attention, but the fact of the matter is, if they can't tell at a glance what your blog, podcast, or website is all about, they probably won't stay.

And how will they know what your blog is about?

Well, your blog name will hopefully give them an idea, but much of the time it is your tagline, along with your main categories and subcategories that will clue them in and let them know, beyond a shadow of a doubt, the exact purpose of your blog, what they can expect to find, and why they should care.

A well-organized home base website is critical for success as an online business owner. Our Blog Structure Blueprint is designed to help you organize the structure and layout of your website so that it 1) makes sense to your readers, 2) allows them to know at a glance what your blog is about, and 3) helps them easily and quickly find what they are looking for.

You can download a printable version of this blueprint at https://eliteblogacademy. com/blogstructureblueprint.

Start with your blog name, followed by your blog's main theme and your tagline. Remember that it is perfectly okay to write about a variety of topics—after all, most of us are not interested in just one single thing—but there does need to be some sort of cohesive overarching theme that ties everything together and prevents your blog from feeling completely random. Random tends to scare people away because they don't know what to expect, and that is not a good thing.

From there, divide your main theme into a few distinct categories, and then divide those categories into subcategories. Keep in mind that the blueprint we've provided is just a guideline for how this might look—there is no rule that you have to have five different categories, and then six subcategories under each category. You might have four categories, and of those four, one might have six subcategories while another has only three, or none at all.

For example, on my website, *Living Well Spending Less*, my main theme and tagline is *Practical Solutions for Everyday Overwhelm*, and I have four main categories—Food Made Simple, Home 101, Life Etc., and Smart Money. If you look at my site, my navigation bar clearly reflects the intentional plan of my blog. If you follow my posts, you will find that 99 percent of the time, the things I write about fall within one of those subtopic categories.

My main theme is pretty broad and includes a lot of things, but it doesn't include *everything*. Thus, my readers know what to expect and they come back because they find practical solutions for everyday life. They would be awfully confused if one day I decided to start doing movie reviews, or if another day I randomly wrote an angry rant about the annoying waitress at a local restaurant.

Even more importantly, with a clear structure in place, I have an easier time writing. When I brainstorm ideas I can look at all my various sub topics and categories to help me narrow down my thoughts and ideas within each group.

Ultimately, your goal is to create a clear, organized structure for your blog, but that can happen in many different ways. The right number of categories and subcategories is the number that it takes for your blog to feel cohesive and organized.

If you are starting a new business from scratch, it's important to give your structure some thought before you even start writing, in order to focus your efforts in one direction and build momentum a whole lot faster.

That said, if you've already started, know that it is never too late to change direction and put a more cohesive structure in place. My own business started in a much different place than it is now. Don't let yourself get trapped by thinking that just because you've always done something one way, you have to continue doing it that way. Map out a plan for your ideal site, figure out what changes you will need to make to get there, and then develop a timeframe for making it happen.

———————

Chapter 1 Action Plan: How to Get Started

- ❏ Brainstorm name & domain name ideas, research availability for URLs & trademarks; pick the best available option.
- ❏ Set up your home base website on either Wordpress.org, Squarespace, or Shopify using the instructions at eliteblogacademy.com/homebase.
- ❏ Get clarity on the two most essential questions—what will you write about, and who are you writing to? Who is your avatar?
- ❏ Determine your main theme or tagline, categories, and subcategories and fill out the blog structure blueprint, which you can download at https://eliteblogacademy.com/blogstructureblueprint.

chapter 2

Content, Content, Content

———————

"I'm just so frustrated! I've spent all this time creating what I think are some pretty amazing products, but no one is buying them! What am I doing wrong? Why can't I ever seem to grow my traffic? And what do I have to do to make more money?!"

JoAnn was almost in tears as she poured out her heart to me during our one-on-one coaching session.

She had been blogging for a long time—years—and she felt like she had been doing all the right things. Her website, playfully called Whimsicle, was beautifully designed, and she had created several products that she was really proud of; including a course on developing your personal style, and one to help parents tame their morning chaos.

The problem? She couldn't seem to get much traffic, her products weren't really selling, and her email list wasn't growing.

She felt completely stuck.

"How often are you posting new content to your blog?" I asked her. "What are you mostly writing about? And who you are writing to?"

JoAnn admitted that she hadn't been posting very often. "I've been so busy working on my courses that I haven't had much time to worry about creating new content for the blog. The only things I've posted lately have been a few sponsored posts, and I don't think those are resonating with my audience."

It was a classic mistake, one that is easy to make. In fact, it's so common that I'd dare say it is the single biggest mistake online business owners make, especially when they're first trying to get their business off the ground.

The mistake? **Doing the right things in the wrong order.**

Every online business owner I know wants more traffic, or more leads, or more customers. Every online business owner I know wants more money and more sales. It's pretty natural to want those things.

But if you want more traffic, more leads, more customers, and more sales, you've got to start with **more content**.

And not just that, you've got to create more of the right content; the content that resonates with your specific avatar, the content that draws them in and keeps them coming back for more, and gets them to know, like, and trust you. Your content is your most powerful marketing tool, but it can only work for you if you are actively working to make it great, and actively working to get more content out there into the world to see which of it is going to stick.

Think, for a minute, about your favorite blog, website, podcast, Instagram feed, or YouTube channel. Not the ones you read or look at occasionally, but the one you can't wait to devour, the ones you find yourself checking even before a new post has a chance to show up in your feed.

What do you love about it? What keeps you coming back day after day?

Is it the cool logo?

Is it the number of subscribers?

Is it the way the website is arranged?

Is it the color of the background or choice of font?

Chances are it is none of those things. Chances are you've barely noticed most of those things for quite some time.

The key to a successful blog is very, very simple: great content, and lots of it.

I dare to bet that your favorite blog, website, or podcast is the one that keeps you interested with an engaging style, thoughtful insights, funny commentary, mouth-watering recipes, creative projects, inspiring ideas for the home, or really anything that makes you want to stop whatever else you are doing and come see what's new, day after day. In other words, your favorite blog has substance and content that rocks.

And in order for *your* blog or website or podcast to be a place that people keep coming back to, and in order for your blog to be popular, successful, and profitable, your substance and content needs to consistently rock as well. You need to keep your audience coming back for more.

CREATE YOUR EDITORIAL CALENDAR

I have plenty of blogger friends who look at me like I have two heads when I start talking about my editorial calendar. They are doing just fine with their post-when-the-mood-strikes approach, thank you very much, and they have no intention of tying themselves down to some arbitrary schedule.

However, I have found that many of them, when pressed, will admit that being unorganized is not always ideal and that they don't always use their time as efficiently as they could. Press them even further and they will probably admit that their blog might be more successful if they were to buckle down and post more regularly, or if they were to devote more time to building traffic and engaging with their readers.

All that to say, if your blog or podcast is already killing it, you're already totally satisfied with your number of page views or downloads, and you're already making all the money you want to make, then by all means, keep doing what you're doing. Keep posting whenever inspiration strikes, or whenever you're in the mood to write or record, or whenever you feel like you have time.

However, for the rest of you, the ones who bought this book in order to grow your blog and eventually profit from it, I can't emphasize enough how important it is from the beginning to get into the regular habit of consistently publishing excellent content. Content that keeps your audience coming back for more, content that allows you to get seen and found by more people, and content that allows your potential customers to get to know, like, and trust you.

And the best way to do that? Create and maintain an editorial calendar.

While an editorial calendar might sound scary or complicated, it really doesn't have to be. Yours might be as simple as a word document with an ongoing list of posts—which is exactly how I used to do it in my early days of blogging.

It looked like this:

MAY EDITORIAL CALENDAR

W-1- Recipe: Black Bean Chili
Th-2-Thrifty Thursday
F-3-Underwritten Post: 7 Ways to Save On Your Next Family Vacation
S-4-NO POST
S-5-Weekend Wandering
M-6-Ditto DIY series Begins!
T-7-Guest Post: Kristen of Joyfully Thriving
W-8-In the Blink of an Eye
Th-9-Thrifty Thursday
F-10-Underwritten Post: DiY Chevron Nail Art
S-11-NO POST

~~S-12-Weekend Wandering~~
~~M-13-DIY: Doll Stroller Replacement Seat HARBOR STYLE ARTICLE DUE-Frugal Family Fun~~
T-14-DIY Stepping Stones
W-15-Recipe: Quick & Easy Chocolate Peanut Butter Oreo Pie
Th-16-Thrifty Thursday
F-17-Things No One Will Tell You About Being a Caregiver (Walgreens)
S-18-NO POST
S-19-Weekend Wandering
M-20-DIY: Rainbow Button iPhone Case
T-21-Guest Post-Sarah {DIY Chevron Rug}
W-22-Blueberry Pie
Th-23-Thrifty Thursday
F-24-The 40 Hanger Closet {Underwritten Post}
S-25-NO POST
S-26-Weekend Wandering
M-27-DIY: Chevron Canvas Wall Art
T-28-NO POST
W-29-The Mermaid Party
Th-30-Thrifty Thursday
F-31-Money Saving iPhone Apps

Once a post was published, it would be crossed out. Posts that were in progress were highlighted in yellow, while posts that were finished and ready to go would get highlighted in green.

These days my team and I use Asana to manage our editorial calendars for both our EBA and LWSL blogs, as well as for the Do It Scared podcast. We like Asana because you can create subtasks under each entry, then duplicate those for each post. This is especially handy if you have multiple people who are responsible for the various subtasks.

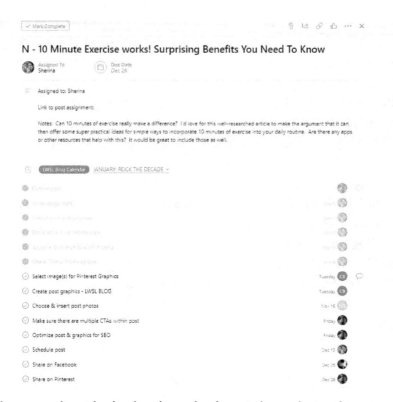

I try to have my editorial calendar planned at least 3-4 months in advance, and have posts ready to go at least 3–4 weeks in advance. Of course it is sometimes necessary to shuffle things around, depending on circumstances, but I have found that having a clear plan for what is coming up allows me to be more efficient with my time.

For home, DIY and food bloggers, maintaining an editorial calendar is especially important! Having an idea of what crafts and recipes you will be sharing over the next few months means you can do all your shopping in one trip, and then spend a day or two crafting or cooking all your posts for the next month, freeing up the rest of your time to edit photos, work on copy, and build traffic. Even if you can afford to hire help, there is a LOT you will still need to do yourself. Work smarter, not harder, in order to maximize your time (something we will talk more about in chapter 11).

Creating and maintaining an editorial calendar allows you to pre-plan for seasonal posts, events, and series, which can end up driving more traffic to your blog. It also gives you the freedom to take a week or two off, whether planned or in an emergency, by having already prepped all your posts for the downtime.

While it might seem overwhelming at first to try to come up with three months of amazing content when you've barely managed a whole week of really great posts so far, it is actually not as difficult as you might think. Really! The key is developing a habit of regular brainstorming sessions. Before you know it, you'll have so many ideas for brilliant content that you'll hardly know where to begin.

EBA CASE STUDY:
Kara Fidd, *Simplifying DIY Design*

Like many first-time moms, Kara Fidd's priorities changed a lot after her son was born. Although she had enjoyed a successful career as a nurse, Kara suddenly realized she didn't want to go back to work full-time. Instead, she wanted to find a way to work from home.

It wasn't easy living on half the income, but she knew she had to make it work. After researching all the different ways of earning money online, Kara decided to start a blog. As it turns out, it wasn't as easy as she thought it would be. There was so much to learn, and she didn't really know where to start.

Then she found Elite Blog Academy.

Working through the course with her first blog, she loved the roadmap and direction EBA provided her. She was no longer wasting time trying to figure it out on her own. Also having a certification in graphic design, Kara discovered she really excelled at the visual aspects of blogging, while she noticed that many other online business owners seemed to struggle with it.

The EBA framework helped her to discover her true niche and launch her second and current website, *Simplifying DIY Design*; created to help bloggers and online business owners overcome their own graphic design struggles.

By recognizing the specific struggles of her readers, then creating solutions to help people overcome those struggles, she has a seemingly never-ending supply of wanted and needed content.

After working the steps, Kara now earns nearly five times what she was making in her old career, and doesn't have to leave the house or pay for daycare! Her family is now able to pay their bills, go on trips, travel and live a completely different life.

START BRAINSTORMING

It's possible that you are reading this book with more content ideas than you know what to do with. Maybe you've been dreaming of starting your blog, podcast, or YouTube channel for a while now, and you're practically bursting at the seams to just get it out there. Or perhaps you've already been blogging for years, and have never had trouble coming up with ideas on what to write about.

If so—that's awesome. Brainstorming won't be a problem for you.

But for the rest of you—the ones who are starting to panic about the idea of having to come up with new ideas of things to write, or the ones for whom the idea side of writing has always been a struggle, this brainstorming exercise is the perfect place to start.

The reality is that learning how to brainstorm effectively in order to generate new ideas is a skill that will serve you well for as long as you have your online business, so you might as well do everything you can to get good at this right away. And while we will specifically be working on brainstorming content ideas right now, this same process can be applied any other time you need new ideas for your business.

Once you've really started working at it, you might just find that the inspired notions and innovative concepts pop up faster than you ever thought possible. That said, it is important to keep in mind that the process of brainstorming—like anything else in life—can take a little practice before it really starts to feel comfortable and before those ideas start flowing naturally. Know ahead of time that it might feel hard and unnatural, and that you might feel frustrated at times when it doesn't seem like the ideas are flowing as quickly as you feel they should.

Resist the urge to get down on yourself if your first few brainstorming sessions are a fail. That is completely NORMAL! Remember—the most important thing that you can do in through this process is to just keep going.

One of my favorite ways to brainstorm content ideas is to take a pad of sticky notes and lay several notes out on my desk—structured like a solitaire game. On the top of each column, I will write down one of my blog's categories or subcategories, and then I will simply start pondering ideas, write them down on a sticky note then add it to the correct category as quickly as I can. When I get stuck in one category, I move on to the next until they are all full. Then I gather up my sticky notes and begin adding the posts to my editorial calendar, shuffling around previously scheduled items as necessary.

Some of my best impromptu brainstorming ideas come while I am cleaning my house. I usually keep a notepad handy on my desk to jot down those ideas as they come.

Finally, I will also sometimes brainstorm on the go using the notepad on my iPhone; usually when I am stuck waiting at the doctor's office or while traveling. I love that my notes get sent straight to my email inbox, where I can then once again, add them to my editorial calendar.

Your own brainstorming sessions might look completely different. You might keep an inspiration binder, or do mind mapping, scour the news for ideas, read magazines or scroll through Pinterest, or maybe go for a long walk or run to clear your brain. There's no one right way to brainstorm, and I recommend trying different strategies to figure out what works best for you, and what helps you to get those ideas flowing. But regardless of what your brainstorming sessions look like, the key is to do them regularly, as often as you can. Trust me, the more you brainstorm, the easier it becomes and the better your content will be for it.

THE DISCIPLINE OF CONTENT CREATION

I'm just going to say this up front: creating great content takes practice.

Whether you are writing blog posts or hosting a podcast or creating videos on YouTube, you will need to work at it. And if your content is terrible, if your writing is filled with grammatical errors, your point isn't clear, or what you have to say doesn't make sense, then you're going to struggle.

Are there exceptions? Of course, but the exceptions usually have something else so awesome people are willing to overlook their less-than-awesome writing.

At this point I'm guessing a few of you may be thinking, "*Well, I've never been a good writer. I hate writing. Clearly I should just quit.*" This is not meant to discourage you or make you want to give up. It is meant to make you work harder.

Writing and content creation is, even for the most naturally gifted writers and communicators, a learned discipline. In 1990 a man named Anders Ericsson did a study that found in order to become an expert at something, you must practice it for at least 10,000 hours, which is the equivalent of practicing twenty hours a week for TEN YEARS. In his book *Outliers: The Story of Success*, Malcolm Gladwell explains that this 10,000-hour requirement is a minimum for anyone truly exceptional. If you want to be a great writer or content creator, you have to practice and practice, and practice some more.

How many of us can say we practice that much?

The thing about becoming a good writer or content creator is that the more you do it, the better you will be. It takes practice. LOTS of practice! It also takes the discipline of actually sitting down at your keyboard to write, not necessarily because you are about to pound out the next great American novel, but because if you don't keep writing, you won't get better.

Don't wait until inspiration strikes; chances are, you'll be waiting a long time. Instead, once you've brainstormed your list of topics, begin to actually start writing those posts. Each morning, evening, or whenever your brain is clearest and your environment is free of distractions, force yourself to write a certain number of words (I like 500) and don't stop until you've met your goal. You'll be amazed at how quickly your writing will improve and how much you are actually able to get done.

If you struggle with grammar and spelling, be sure to have someone edit for you—at least for a while. Consider joining a writing group, either online or in real life, so that you can get honest feedback and constructive criticism.

My husband proofreads almost everything I write, and I honestly don't know what I would do without him. He catches the little spelling mistakes that my brain skips over and that spell-check doesn't always pick up on. He also lets me know when something doesn't flow right or if something doesn't quite make sense. His feedback is invaluable.

HOW TO CREATE CONTENT THAT ROCKS

Once you are determined to sit down and just pound it out, it is time to get going on your first killer piece of content—one that your readers will really respond to. A truly fantastic and compelling piece of content, whether it be a blog post, email, podcast episode or video, usually means more traffic, more comments, more pins on Pinterest, more tweets, and more Facebook shares; all of which will help grow your platform.

But what makes content that rocks? Your killer content can and should:

Make a clear point. Compelling content almost always has a clear takeaway or message that can be boiled down to one short sentence. If you, the author, aren't able to summarize your point, how will the reader be expected to follow your logic? Always write with the point in mind. If you have multiple points, split it into two posts.

Evoke an emotional response. The content that people tend to remember (and share) is the content that makes them feel a certain way, whether that be happy, angry, encouraged, or inspired. This means they usually take a stand one way or another. Neutral might seem safe, but it is boring and forgettable.

Be easy to read or listen to. Blog posts should be clear and concise. Statistics show that blog readers tend to skim, so use short paragraphs, headers, and bullet points. It is okay—essential even—to write conversationally, but proper grammar and spelling is mandatory. Always. Likewise, your audio or video content should be clear, concise, and easy to listen to and understand.

Teach a simple lesson. Whether your post or video is a DIY tutorial showing how to make something, a recipe, or some other helpful tip, the best blog posts stick to one clear and easy-to-follow lesson. This is not to say you can't do complicated projects or recipes, but I can guarantee that the projects with the best response will be the simplest of the bunch.

Stir up controversy. Often the best, most compelling content takes a clear stand and forces the reader to have a reaction one way or another. The stronger their stance, the more intense the reaction will be. Of course don't be controversial just for the sake of stirring up controversy! Readers can sniff inauthenticity a mile away. If there is a particular topic you truly feel strongly about, don't try to come off as neutral. Neutral is boring. Just be prepared for people to disagree with you!

Be visually appealing. Compelling blog posts need compelling images to go with them and help tell the story. With the advent of Pinterest, this is not only important for recipes and DIY, but for ALL articles. I can't tell you how many awesome articles I haven't pinned because there was no image to go with it. We will talk a LOT more about this later!

Not be overly complicated. Don't use large words when a small word will suffice. I once heard Tsh Oxenreider from TheArtofSimple.net say that her pet peeve is when someone uses the word *utilize* when *use* means the exact same thing in all situations. I don't think I have used *utilized* since!

Make you say WOW. What's your awesome factor? Whatever you share, whether it be a recipe, a party, an idea, or a project, it should be so compelling that your reader or listener can't help but stop whatever they are doing and pay attention. If it's not great, don't bother. You are better off sharing one WOW post a month than twenty forgettable ones.

Empower your audience. Compelling content isn't about YOU or what you've done, created, or cooked. Yes, you may be sharing something you've done, or stories about your own experience, but the best content does this only in a way that allows the audience to relate the story or experience to their own life.

Be unique and interesting. Compelling content has something new to say, even for topics that have been addressed over and over. It presents a unique viewpoint or an interesting perspective—your unique viewpoint or perspective. It gives your audience a different way of looking at a problem that perhaps they hadn't considered before, and it is fresh and sharp.

Keep in mind that not all of these tips must, or even should be used in one piece of content, but generally the more of them that you can hit, the better off you will be.

CREATE YOUR PILLAR CONTENT

Building a successful online platform requires creating as much compelling pillar content as you can. Your goal should be to knock it out of the park and create a killer piece of share-worthy content every single time. After all, your time is precious. As a small business owner, you will almost always have more to do than you actually have time for, which means there is really no point in wasting your time creating content that is just okay.

At Elite Blog Academy, I teach a method for content creation called FOCUS that has helped my students—even the ones who are scared of writing—create consistently stellar content by giving them a clear but simple framework to follow.

FOCUS is an acronym that stands for First Impression, Opening, Central Idea, Useful Logic & Illustrations, and Strong Conclusion. Using this framework every time you create a piece of content will help to make sure each piece of content serves the purpose of growing your tribe of raving fans.

To learn more on how to exactly create consistently stellar content with FOCUS, watch my free bonus training video at https://eliteblogacademy.com/focustraining, which will walk you through the entire FOCUS process.

Your pillar content will be those posts or episodes that ultimately draw the most traffic to your blog, podcast, or website, and the content that helps you build your tribe of raving fans. It's the content that people remember. The content that gets lots of comments, pins, social shares, and that is easily optimized for great search engine traffic.

Generally, the more pillar content you can create, the more you can figure out what actually resonates with your audience, and the faster you'll be able to grow your audience and potential customer base.

This is certainly what happened for JoAnn.

After realizing that she had been doing the right things in the wrong order, JoAnn decided to go back to the basics and focus solely on creating pillar content that would resonate with her avatar.

She began publishing new blog posts three times a week, making sure to optimize each one for search engine results and social sharing. She began paying attention to which of those posts were resonating the strongest with her audience, which were bringing in the most traffic, and she started creating more of what she called "spin-off" posts that also resonated with her readers.

But not only that, by paying attention to what was resonating with her audience, she was better equipped to understand how to serve her people. She even rebranded, changing the name of her site from Whimsicle to No Guilt Mom, and began narrowing her focus to help moms equip their kids to be more self-sufficient.

It worked.

Within months—after years of struggling to get traction—her traffic skyrocketed, to the tune of 200,000+ page views per month, and her email list started to grow as well. Suddenly she had an audience of raving fans excited about buying her products, which meant a whole lot more income as well.

That's the power of content marketing, and that's exactly how it can work for your business too.

Chapter 2 Action Plan: Create Consistently Stellar Content

❑ Create and begin using an editorial calendar.

❑ Schedule a brainstorming session at least once a month.

❑ Practice, practice, practice—your ability to create amazing content will only improve with practice.

❑ Focus on publishing as many pieces of pillar content as you can, then pay attention to what's resonating. Do more of what works and less of what doesn't.

chapter 3

Your Pretty Package

———————

"I can't believe this lady is talking about organizing. Her blog might be the ugliest, most cluttered and unorganized website I've ever seen."

Talk about brutal honesty.

It was 2012, and it was, to that point, the harshest comment I had ever received, one I can only assume the author never intended for me to see. I happened to stumble upon it in a thread on Facebook where someone had shared my most recent blog post; an article I had written about organizing, decluttering, or getting your life in order, and there was one comment that stood out like it was written in flashing red letters.

It was a dagger straight to my soul.

And I'm not going to lie, I may have shed more than a few tears over that less-than-gentle nugget of feedback. I had been working so hard, for more than two years at that point. I wanted so badly to make this blogging thing work and to make my business a success that I was getting up at 3am every single day, and sometimes even earlier, just to try and keep up. I was trying everything I could, and here was this random mean girl on the internet who could just tear me down and rip me apart, without a second thought.

But the thing is… she was RIGHT.

While the term 'ugly' might be a little subjective, the reality is that in 2012, my website was a cluttered and chaotic MESS, filled with too many colors, too many patterns, and just too much of everything all at the same time. I hadn't narrowed my focus, figured out who I was writing to, or even what I wanted to say—which meant that I was all over the place. And this meant that my blog was all over the place. How was anyone supposed to find their way around, or even know what my site was all about?

My content might have been incredible, but it didn't matter because of the way it was being presented. My packaging was a disaster. The busy design didn't fit the content, and my business was floundering.

But I couldn't see it. I was so deep in the weeds of trying to get somewhere, that I had no perspective. And it took a super harsh comment from some random mean-girl-on-the-Internet to allow me to finally see what everyone else saw.

Here is the brutal truth: you can write the best, most interesting, most compelling articles in the whole world, but if the package doesn't sell it, you are doomed. If your site design is garish or obviously looks like you did it yourself, or if your graphics are ugly, your navigation frustrating, or your images are poor quality, most people will turn away before they even give you a chance.

And so, after several months of licking my wounds and pondering the situation, I finally decided that she might be at least partially right. I contacted my blog designer and together we came up with a design that was simple, organized, and easy to navigate, with fewer colors and more white space.

My traffic started climbing almost overnight, not just a little bit, but dramatically! I started getting a lot more traffic to older posts because with the new navigation, people could actually find what they were looking for, and all the fantastic pillar content that I had worked so hard to create was finally being read, pinned and shared.

Presentation is everything.

So thank you, random mean girl, wherever you are. I totally owe you one.

GET SOME PERSPECTIVE (AND SOME HONEST FEED-BACK)

While we might like to think that we are all our own worst critics, the reality is that it is often hard to get perspective on your own work; especially when it comes to content marketing. The biggest problem is that we know what we're trying to achieve, and so rather than see the holes in our design or structure or layout, our brain simply fills them in. We become blind to the mistakes and shortcomings, and we can't really see where things might be confusing or unclear.

And that's why it is so important to get a little perspective—ideally someone else's perspective—and to get some honest feedback. Your goal is for your readers and potential customers, to understand—within the first few seconds of landing on your site—what your blog or business is about, and what they can expect to gain from being there.

If you've been at this for a while and already have a fully completed website in place, this is the time to take a step back and look at it from a critics point of view. Even if you spent money on a professional design, even if you *just* got it all set up, be brutally, and painfully honest.

Ask yourself the following questions:

- Is some aspect of your design holding you back? Is it too cluttered, too garish, or too confusing?

- Does your navigation make perfect sense? Can your visitors find what they are looking for?
- Does your design tell newcomers, at first glance, what your blog or business is about? Would they be able to tell in thirty seconds the main types of posts on your site, and would they know how to find them?
- Are your graphics crisp and clean? Do they use appealing, high-quality images?
- Are your fonts easy to read?
- Is there a clear call to action? Do your readers know what you want them to do or where you want them to go?

Try to look at your site with the eyes of a stranger. Pretend you are going in completely blind, and that you don't have any idea what your website is supposed to be about, or how to find things. Pretend that you're not at all tech-savvy. Does it still make sense? Is your message clear?

From there, I recommend reaching out to a few friends, colleagues, or family members—preferably those who are similar to your avatar—and ask for some honest feedback. You could set up a Google form, or simply give them a sheet to use that includes the following questions:

- Do you understand what this website is about?
- What do you like about the design? What don't you like?
- Does the navigation make sense? Can you find what you are looking for?
- Do you understand where I want you to go?
- What stands out the most to you?
- Are the fonts & graphics appealing and easy to read?
- What would you change?

Another great way to get an unbiased opinion is to use a user-testing service, such as UserBob[4]. While this service is not free, it is relatively inexpensive, and can be a great way to see your site through the eyes of a stranger.

The ultimate goal with all of this feedback, of course, is to then actually apply what you've learned to improve your design and layout, in order to improve your user experience. And when it comes to improving your design, there are a few key areas you'll want to focus on: structure & navigation, the overall look & feel, and the images and graphics you use to tell a visual story.

STICK TO A CLEAR STRUCTURE

In Chapter 1, we talked about the importance of establishing a clear structure for your blog or website. You determined exactly what you planned to write about, and then you developed your main site theme, your categories, and your subcategories, using our EBA Blog Structure Blueprint tool found at www.eliteblogacademy.com/blogstructureblueprint.

So what are you supposed to do with that structure?

You use it to structure your navigation. Your website's navigation should make it easy to find the things you are writing or posting about in a way that makes sense to even the most casual and inexperienced reader. If it doesn't, if your posts are hard to find, or your structure doesn't make sense or it feels unorganized, you need to change it.

For the record, creating cohesive navigation that ensures a great experience for the reader does NOT magically happen on its own. It is something that you will have to intentionally work at to make sure all your posts are categorized correctly, and that your categories, your subcategories, and your overall navigation makes sense. Even if you are working with a designer, they will not be responsible for deciding what those categories and subcategories are going to be—you will.

Here's why: no one knows your content like you. Take the time to create main categories that capture the topics you plan to write about, and to create subcategories that fit underneath those main categories. Make sure every post is categorized, and then eliminate categories that don't fit. Once everything is categorized the way it should be, make sure your navigation bar is clear, concise, and easy to—you guessed it—navigate.

Next, take the time to make sure your very best content is highlighted in a way that stands out to people, and make it available to them in as many ways as you can. Did you write a killer series or e-book? Make a button for your sidebar that highlights it AND make it a category in your navigation bar. Do you have a few awesome posts that readers love? Make a popular post page AND add a "most popular posts" section to your sidebar.

Above all, make sure it makes sense. Ask a few honest friends or family members—preferably ones that don't spend much time on your site—to critique your navigation. Could they find what they were looking for? What were they drawn to? What turned them off? Then, once you've gotten an honest look at what is wrong, fix the problems!

KEEP IT CLEAN AND SIMPLE

As a general rule, the best website designs are also the simplest. Essentially, your web design should include the bare minimum of what people need to be able to find the content they are looking for, and it should lead your visitors down a specific path—one that you design—so that they are compelled to take the action you want them to take.

Yes, of course you want your blog design to reflect your personality, but in order to showcase your content and not detract from it, your overall design should not command all the attention. When in doubt, less is more, so keep it understated. The most important thing to remember is that an amazing design won't keep people if the content stinks, but a bad or overly busy design will turn people away, even if the content is amazing.

Your design should be the tasteful packaging, the pretty wrapping paper that makes people want to unwrap the gift to see what's inside.

Here are a few "clean" website designs I love from a few of our students at Elite Blog Academy:

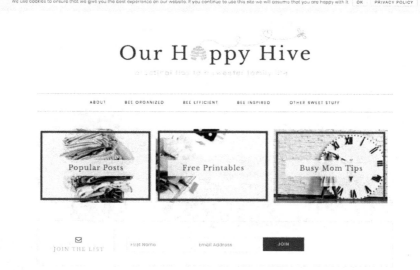

Melissa James: Our Happy Hive

Stephanie Miller: The Scenic Suitcase

CHEAP CHRISTMAS GIFTS FOR YOUNG GIRLS

Posted on November 21, 2019 by Amber Masters

Hi there! I'm Amber! And welcome to the Deeply

Amber Masters: Deeply in Debt

Kelly Winzer: Mindfully Mad

And then of course there is my own blog at *Living Well Spending Less*, which is much simpler and a big improvement from my previous design:

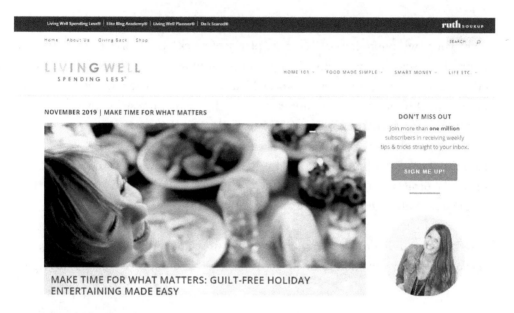

You'll notice that none of these websites look anything alike, nor are any of them "blah". A clean and simple site means the content is what shows through. Between advertising, social media buttons, subscription boxes, and blog posts, every single site is full of information overload. Do your readers a favor and keep it simple.

TELL A VISUAL STORY

I cannot emphasize enough just how important it is to tell a visual story with your written content. With the rise of social media, the online world has become increasingly visual, while attention spans have gotten shorter and shorter. Adding photos to your written content that help break up the text and tell the story will not only make your content more interesting and easier to read, but more likely to get noticed and shared.

Just like a beautiful design won't save your blog but a bad design will sink it, beautiful images will enhance and help you promote the amazing content that is already there, while poor-quality pictures will mean no one even takes the time to look.

Of course, depending on the subject matter of your blog, you don't necessarily have to take your own photographs. There are plenty of stock photo services available that can provide gorgeous, compelling imagery for your blog. The downside is that most of these services charge for their photos, which can get expensive quickly. In addition to the original photos we use on our website, we frequently use stock images from stock photo sites such as 123rf.com and istockphoto.com.

That said, if you are a home, DIY, craft or food blogger, or even if you do an occasional DIY project or recipe on your blog, you will be well served to learn as much as you can about photography, staging, and photo editing.

There is far too much to say about photography to include in this book, but here are a few quick general tips that can help get you started and improve your photos right away:

Your camera matters. If you plan to take a lot of photos for your blog, you may want to invest in at least a starter DSLR camera, and consider also investing in a premium lens. That said, smartphone cameras have gotten really, really good over the past few years, and a high-quality smartphone can give you results that are almost as good as a DSLR.

Get the lighting right. There is nothing more important to a photograph than good lighting! In fact, learning about photography is more about learning to understand light than anything else. Bright, indirect daylight is best. If you are shooting food or crafts, shoot during the day, either outside, in the shade, or in front of a well-lit window with your back to the window. Make sure you are out of the direct sunlight! Whenever possible, avoid using your flash.

Check your background. Make sure there is nothing weird or distracting in your background. The plainer, the better.

Use the "Rule of Thirds." For better composition, use the grid setting in your phone's camera to split the photo into thirds horizontally and vertically, then try to get the main focal point of your photo to be on one of the lines, or at one of the four intersecting points.

There are lots of great online resources for learning how to work your camera, regardless of what type of camera you decide to choose. For a full list of our latest recommendations, check out our resources page at eliteblogacademy.com/resources.

Of course, it is also possible that your topic or niche doesn't lend itself to images at all, whether they be stock photos or original photography. So what do you do then? This was a problem we experienced with our Elite Blog Academy blog, so we switched to using vector illustrations instead of images, which was hugely successful.

MAKE IT SHARE-WORTHY

Rest assured we'll be talking a lot more about how to grow your audience before this book is done. In fact, the next part of this book is fully devoted to that very topic. But for now, while we're talking specifically about the way you package your content and the visual aspects of your brand and website, we need to spend a few minutes talking specifically about Pinterest.

Because while Pinterest is not the "magical" traffic tool that it was a few years ago, it is still a powerful way to help drive traffic, particularly if you haven't yet established a platform. That means that it is worth spending some time on to get it right.

The great thing about spending the time to make your content "pin-worthy" is that doing so actually makes your content better. Pin-worthy content is also share-worthy via other social media outlets, and more SEO friendly as well. In fact, I like to think of Pinterest as more of a visual search engine than a social media channel.

So what makes content pin-worthy? Pay attention now because this part is important: **the most pin-worthy posts are the perfect combination of compelling**

content and highly shareable images.

In the last chapter, we talked a lot about the importance of creating consistently stellar content. Stellar content is compelling. Stellar content makes people want to click over *right then and there*. Stellar content then makes those readers re-pin, share and comment, which in turn convinces other readers to do the same. **Stellar content sells itself.**

But Pinterest is a *visual* search engine, which means that the accompanying image to your stellar content *must* be equally compelling. Your image must sell your content. In other words, the image you pin should tell enough of your story to make people want to read more.

There have been a few studies on what types of pins get noticed, shared and pinned. These observations from Curalate Insights[5] are a good place to start:

- Colorful images are better than monochromatic images.
- Bright images are better than dark images.
- Warm colors are more likely to be re-pinned than cool colors.
- Close-up shots are more likely to be re-pinned than panoramic shots.
- Pins without faces are far more likely to be re-pinned.

At this point you may be thinking something like, *"well, my content isn't about crafts or home decor or recipes, so Pinterest doesn't really apply to me."*

It doesn't matter.

In fact, my own anecdotal research and personal experience on Pinterest has found that while recipes and DIY images do tend to get re-pinned quite a bit, they don't drive nearly as much blog traffic as articles and images that relate to something interesting, helpful, inspirational, or life-changing.

People will pin and collect images they like, simply because they are pretty, interesting, inspiring, or because they look delicious. Converting those pins to page views means taking your beautiful images one or two steps further. Those images must correspond to great content, and your image description on Pinterest must be engaging enough to capture people's attention and give them enough of a sense of urgency to want to read that post right then and there.

This means, if you are a DIY, home decor, or food blogger, your beautiful images must connect on an emotional level or they will simply be re-pinned without really driving traffic. On the other hand, if you are a writer, this means making your accompanying image compelling enough to sell your story, similarly to the way a book cover sells its content.

We'll be talking more about how to best leverage Pinterest in Chapter 5, but in the meantime, to give you a better idea of what I am talking about, here are a few examples of some popular pins from my own websites, as well as from some of our Elite Blog Academy students. All of the following pins have been pinned and re-pinned thousands of times, and have driven tens of thousands of new readers to my blog. Notice that they represent a variety of subjects, from recipes to cleaning tips to DIY projects and beyond. But each one has three important things in common: great content, a nice image and graphic that works with the title, and a compelling description to make you want to click and read that post.

 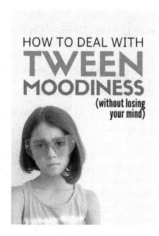 

In the end, it really is a very simple formula:

Stellar Content + Compelling Image + Engaging Description = More Traffic.

Sounds good, doesn't it? And with that in mind, it's time to start thinking about growing your traffic.

Chapter 3 Action Plan: Refine Your Presentation

- ❏ Do an honest assessment of your current blog design. Ask for feedback from as many people as you can, then make a plan for what to change.
- ❏ Create an organized, well-thought-out structure for your website that is reflected in your navigation.
- ❏ Keep your design clean, simple, and free of unnecessary extras.
- ❏ Begin telling a visual story with your content and create share-worthy graphics for every post.

PHASE 2 | GROW

Once you've nailed down your messaging, your next step is to start growing your audience. After all, if you're going to have a business, you're going to need customers—your own loyal tribe of raving fans, and a group of people who know, like, and trust you. Because once you've got that, selling to them is the easy part!

In this section, we'll start by reviewing all the different ways to start growing your audience, both free and paid, along with the pros and cons of each one. From there, we'll talk about why growing your email list is the most important growth metric you can focus on, as well as talk about how to re-think your growth strategy on social media (and stop chasing vanity metrics). By the end of this section, you should have a solid plan in place for getting more eyes on your page.

chapter 4

How to Get Found Online

———————

"How do I get more traffic?"
"How are people supposed to find me?"
"How do I get more page views?"
"Where do I find more customers?"

Nothing is more daunting to the new blogger or online business owner than the thought of finding people who are actually interested in what you have to say. After all, it's one thing to start creating content and putting it out there for the world to see. It's a whole other thing to actually invite people to start consuming that content.

And it almost feels like a mystery—where does all this traffic come from? How are people supposed to find your website (or your podcast or YouTube channel for that matter)? How do you grow a tribe of people who know, like, and trust you?

Well, first you have to know where to look.

The truth is that growing your traffic is not the giant mystery it sometimes seems to be. There's no big secret that people are keeping from you, nor is there some magic formula that you haven't figured out yet.

In fact, all traffic growth strategies can be divided into two main categories—organic and paid.

The main benefit of using organic growth strategies is that they're free—you don't have to pay to play, which can feel like a pretty appealing option when you're starting with a tiny (or even non-existent) budget. Your only real investment is time. The downside of organic growth is that it tends to be pretty slow. You've got to be patient, because all that growth doesn't happen overnight. It takes weeks and months and sometimes years to build momentum, and sometimes it can feel like nothing is actually happening, which can be frustrating.

The benefit of paid growth strategies is that they tend to work a lot faster, and they're more predictable; which gives you a much better measure of control in your business. You're not waiting and hoping that the actions you take will eventually pay off organically—you're paying for results. Of course, the downside of paid growth is that it costs a lot more (obviously), but with increased costs, there are increased risks. It can take time to hone in on a paid growth strategy that actually works, which can be a little scary when you feel like you're spending money on something that's not working.

As an online business owner, one of the first decisions you're going to have to make when it comes to growing your audience is whether to focus on organic growth (which will be less risky but will generally mean a slower trajectory), or whether to focus on paid growth (which will allow you to grow faster with more predictability, but will mean taking a bigger risk).

But before I delve into the details of these two different growth strategies, I have to start with a strong word of caution, as I know there are probably more than a few readers who will come straight to this chapter without bothering to read about the importance of content and presentation first. Are you ready? **Don't try to grow your audience if your message isn't ready.** Just don't do it.

There really is no point in trying to build your online business if your content is just okay, your navigation is an exercise in frustration, your do-it-yourself website design screams amateur, and your poor-quality images are completely uninspiring. Yes, maybe your parents will read it and love everything you have to say, but the rest of the world will pass.

Always keep in mind that **sustainable traffic growth only happens if your content rocks.** Getting people to come once is one thing; getting them to come back again and again (then tell all their friends to come too) is what will ultimately build your online business. If you are working like crazy to build your traffic and you aren't seeing any results, it might be time to go back to the drawing board and re-evaluate your content.

But now, with that lecture out of the way, let's look at each of these two growth strategies in more detail.

EBA CASE STUDY:
Sarah Morris, *The Tudor Travel Guide*

Sarah Morris is really passionate about two things: travel and history.

And so, when it came to starting a business, she knew that she wanted to find a way to combine her two great loves. After starting with Elite Blog Academy, her brilliant idea for *The Tudor Travel Guide* was born—a place where she could help her readers and customers connect with the history of the locations they happened to be visiting.

Although she had a different website prior to starting EBA, it had basically gone dormant because she never knew how to grow it. But once she started EBA, she consistently worked on new and different ways to drive traffic, get more eyes on her page, and she also began to understand that as long as you are taking action, you are not failing; even if you are not initially seeing the results as quickly as you had hoped for.

In fact, Sarah quickly learned that understanding what does NOT work, is every bit as important as what does work—which is exactly how she has gotten to where she is! She took the time and paid attention to what was working in terms of SEO, Pinterest, and other growth channels, and started doing more of what works and less of what didn't.

The first real signs of results came in just six months after starting EBA. While her numbers started growing, they quickly began doubling volume in terms of visitors and page views. And, because she operates in a very specific niche, the SEO work she did through EBA started to yield results pretty quickly. Her page began appearing on the first page on Google for several different search topics related to her niche.

After just 6 months, she had grown her email list to over 1,200 subscribers, her message was resonating, and she was well on her way to creating the business of her dreams!

ORGANIC GROWTH STRATEGIES

For those of you who are risk averse and started having heart palpitations the minute I mentioned advertising, the good news is that there are plenty of relatively effective ways you can start growing your audience and driving traffic to your site without spending a single dollar on advertising.

But one thing that's important to remember is that organic growth strategies are constantly changing. What worked well five years ago now seems archaic, and what works now may very well be just a flash in the pan. In fact, it's one of the main reasons this book is now in its third edition—much of what was working during the last edition no longer applies.

So why bother with organic methods at all, you might be wondering, if the internet and social media are changing so fast? The answer is that when you are trying to grow an online business, it's smart to start by getting traffic any and every way you can. While paid traffic—which we will talk about in a few minutes—can be faster and more predictable, it's also more expensive. I have learned the hard way that it is never a good idea to put all your eggs in one basket. The more diverse your streams of traffic, the more stable your business will be.

The smartest approach to growing your audience is to work on traffic from a variety of angles, in however many ways you can, focusing on both short-term gains and long-term growth.

Word of Mouth

Quite honestly, this is how many online business owners got their start, and how most continue on the path to online business success. You start a blog or a website, post a few things, then tell a few friends, or a few family members who in turn—if what you're sharing is any good—share with a few more friends and extended family members, and so on and so on.

Word of mouth is actually a great way to start growing your audience, and to start getting feedback from people you know and trust. They can tell you if you are on the right track (or what needs work) before you try marketing yourself to the masses. Telling the people you know that you are writing a blog or starting a business is also critical practice; after all, if you can't sell to your best friend, then to whom can you sell?

Before you go out and start telling people, put some time and thought into crafting your "elevator pitch"—your thirty-second overview of what your business is about, and why people should be interested (i.e. what's in it for them)! Practice it, hone it, and OWN it. Then go out and let people know!

If you are in the beginning stages of launching your business, or even if you've been working on it for a while but haven't quite dared to tell those closest to you, here are a few ideas:

→ Send a quick email to everyone in your address book, inviting them all to read your latest (or favorite) blog post. Be sure to include the link! If you're feeling brave, let them know you would love to get some honest feedback, then ask a few specific questions. Just be sure you're prepared for honesty!

→ Every single time you publish a blog post, share it with a comment on your personal Facebook page. Again, ask for feedback!

→ Have inexpensive business cards printed, then share them with everyone you know.

→ Have an inexpensive bumper sticker or car decal printed with your web address. This is how all my neighbors—even the ones I didn't know—started reading my blog! (A word of caution—depending on what you write about, that can get weird. Sometimes it is better that your neighbors don't know about your blog.)

→ Politely ask the people you trust who you know read (and like) your blog to spread the word. You can do this via a blog post, or at the end of each blog post, or in person.

It is easy to feel embarrassed at first when you are promoting your blog or online business. Maybe you're afraid your friends will mock you or think your ideas are silly. Perhaps you just aren't quite confident that anything you've written is worth reading. In all honesty, your friends might mock you—mine certainly did when I first started! Worse yet, your blog might actually not be worth reading, at least not yet. However, if you don't face your fears and learn how to promote yourself from the very start, beginning with the people who know you best, you will probably never be able to build a successful blogging business. At the end of the day, YOU will always be your best marketer, and this will be true whether you have ten readers or ten thousand readers.

I personally think it is helpful to look at it a different way. If you were starting a brick-and-mortar business, you would be darn sure to tell every single person you knew about that business, and then you would ask those people to tell everyone they knew, and so on. You wouldn't stop telling people, because your livelihood would depend on it!

If you think of your blog as a business, even before it makes a dime, telling people (and improving your product through early market research) stops feeling like shameless self-promotion and a whole lot more like the thing you do when you believe in something.

Commenting on Other Websites

In the first few months of starting my online business, I read as many books and articles as I could about the subject of growing blog traffic, and everything I read said "leave comments on bigger websites within your same genre." I took this advice to heart and became a very frequent commenter on a few of my favorite blogs and websites, sometimes leaving as many as five or ten comments a day.

In my defense, most of my comments were thoughtful and helpful and genuinely contributed to the post conversation, and, to be fair, all those comments did drive a lot of traffic to my blog, especially from the one blog I commented on most often. However, I have to admit that more than a few times my "helpful" comments crossed the line into somewhat spammy, shameless self-promotion territory.

While the traffic was nice, and I do in fact recommend commenting on bigger blogs as a great way to build traffic, I don't recommend becoming that girl (or guy).

I learned that lesson the hard way when five minutes into my first blogging conference, I bumped into that blogger I had been spam-stalking for several months, and, upon telling her my blog name, she said, "Oh, I know who you are. You leave a lot of comments on my blog." At that moment I pretty much wanted to sink into the floor and die, and I can guarantee you that I have never spammed another blog since!

That blogger and I have since become friends and I can now laugh about my over-zealousness. That said, I did learn an important lesson, one that is even more apparent now that I have been blogging for long enough to be the target of more than a few spammy blog comments myself.

The lesson is that while bloggers pretty much universally love to get comments, and while most seasoned bloggers don't mind helping newbies when they can, trying to "scam" the traffic that those bloggers worked incredibly hard for just isn't a good practice. It could even get you banned from a site, or, as in my case, end up being one of your most embarrassing and truly cringe-worthy blogging moments ever.

A much better approach is to read blogs you like—particularly ones that would have great crossover traffic—and if a post genuinely moves or inspires you, leave a thoughtful comment with your website URL in the appropriate box. You can even have your name be YourName@YourWebsiteName, and as long as your comment is genuine and insightful, it won't come across like spam or shameless self-promotion. On the contrary, depending on what you have to say, it might just spur quite a few people to go check out you and your blog.

Networking and Collaboration

The opportunity to meet and collaborate with other entrepreneurs and online business owners is without question my very favorite part of having an online business. I can say without hesitation that I count many of my online friends among my nearest and dearest, and that I am a better person for having known them.

Aside from the personal benefits, forging genuine friendships with other entrepreneurs has opened so many doors for me. It has given me the opportunity to partner and collaborate with some amazing people, which has in turn helped grow my business. I can honestly say that almost every fantastic opportunity I've had has come from a personal connection I've made.

Conferences and in-person meetups, or masterminds, are by far the best way I've found to connect with other online business owners. There is really something so amazing and inspiring about being in a room full of people who "get it"—this crazy, misunderstood profession we call entrepreneurship—and if you are willing to put yourself out there, even a little, you are almost certain to find at least one or two kindred spirits in the crowd. In fact, these days my main purpose for attending conferences is most often just the chance to connect. I almost always get more out of the late-night gab sessions and conversations in the hallways than from the actual sessions themselves.

Here are a few tips to (hopefully) make connecting with other bloggers at your first (or next) blog conference a little easier:

> **Focus on connections.** You'll be tempted to try to attend every session to "maximize" your investment. Resist that temptation. Attend the sessions that really appeal to you, but don't be afraid to skip a session in favor of going out for coffee with the gals you met at breakfast, or to sleep in because you stayed up half the night chatting with the roommate you just met.

> **Find a roommate.** If you are going to your first conference by yourself, try to find a roommate. Most blogging conferences have Facebook groups with a roommate connection thread—use it! Even if you and your roommate don't ultimately become BFFs, there is something comforting about knowing at least one other person in the crowd.

> **Engage, don't card swap.** There is seriously no bigger turn-off than having someone hand you their card before they've even said hello. I honestly don't even bother keeping the cards of people I haven't had an actual conversation with. And when in doubt of what to say, ask a question!

Listen more than you speak. Before I head off to any conference, my (older and wiser) husband always tells me, "Remember, honey, you have two ears and one mouth." It is his gentle way of reminding me that I tend to talk a lot when I get nervous, but that the way to best connect with people is to ask questions and genuinely listen to the answers. It is also the best way to learn!

Foster your friendships. If you are lucky enough to connect with one or two people in a real and authentic way, don't let that friendship fade out before it has a chance to truly bloom. Start reading the blogs of the people you met, and leave comments so they know you were there. Send an occasional tweet or text message just to say hi. Connect on Facebook. In other words, be a friend!

Guest Posting

Guest posts, when done well, can be a fantastic way to gain exposure and drive traffic to your site. The key to a successful guest post is not only posting on a site with a similar audience, but to write something so good that your host's readers will want to check out your site to read more.

At *Living Well Spending Less*, we host a lot of guest contributors, but as anyone who has written a guest post for my site will attest, I am extremely picky about who we choose. First of all, you must be an EBA student to even be considered. And then, even after a post topic has been approved, I almost always send the post back for at least one revision by the author, and sometimes multiple revisions, until I feel that it is the right fit for my audience.

And while all those requirements might sound like a whole lot of work (because they are), I believe that the benefits of guest posting on my site makes it worth the extra effort. First of all, I promote my guest posts just like I would any other pillar content post on my site. They get re-promoted via social media on a regular basis and continue to drive a steady stream of traffic long after the post has been published. The better and more popular the post, the more I promote it and the more traffic it generates.

If you are interested in guest posting for larger sites, here are a few additional tips to keep in mind:

Ask for guest-post guidelines. Many large websites get dozens of requests each week for accepting guest content. While I can't speak for anyone else, I can say that of the requests that come in to LWSL, close to 95 percent get deleted immediately, simply because they look like spam or the author is very obviously trying to promote a product or business. Before offering a list of prefabricated posts, instead try asking for a copy of the site's guest post guidelines to be sure that your post is a good fit for that particular site.

Only submit original content. Most sites will require that the post submitted is 100 percent original. Yes, that means more work for you. That's just part of the deal.

Don't be overly familiar. As a guest poster, you are writing to a new audience, not your own. Don't use cutesy terms or slang, or refer to the readers as "friends." Instead, maintain a slightly more formal version of your own voice than you would use on your own blog. Furthermore, don't assume this audience will understand a term you've written about before, or that they will click your link to read more. Your guest post should not require further explanation.

Don't make your post self-promotional. Yes, you want your post to drive traffic to your site, but filling your post with links will only annoy your host and their readers. One or two relevant links are probably okay, but more than that is inappropriate.

Submit your BEST content. Don't waste time with guest posts if you are not also willing to make your guest posts really, really, really good. While I can't speak for other sites, I can say that when a guest post on my site is really good, I add it to the rotation of my other pillar content and continue to promote it via social media indefinitely. This means that it will continue to drive traffic to those sites for months and years to come. Of course, if the post is just okay, I will either not publish it at all or simply let it fade away into the archives. A great guest post provides value to the reader and keeps them coming back for more!

EBA CASE STUDY:
Julianna Poplin, *The Simplicity Habit*

There's nothing Julianna loves more than simplifying, decluttering and organizing. Except, perhaps, writing and helping other people simplify, declutter, and get organized.

And so, when it came time to start an online business, Julianna knew her sweet spot would be helping her readers and customers find simple ways to manage all aspects of their life.

For her, blogging was practically a no-brainer, especially since it seemed to encompass all of those things she loves. Even so, she was having some trouble getting eyes on her site. She felt like she was trying to do too many things at once, and even noted that at times she was NOT following the framework, and knew her focus was not in the right order.

She knew if she was going to be serious about building this business, that she was going to need to take a step back and return to the EBA framework and implement what she is learning.

So that's exactly what she did. She took a step back, began focusing on content, and began submitting guest posts to other blogs. She immediately starting see the results in the forms of spikes in traffic which even led to one of her posts going viral!

At the same time, she focused on growing her email list and converting those casual readers into loyal raving fans. And now, her business keeps growing because Julianna is focused on creating awesome content and getting it in front of as many eyes as possible, but also following through and optimizing those new leads coming to her site. It's a perfect example of not only why staying focused on your content is so important, but also why it is so essential to share your content on other platforms and have a clear call to action when they come to you!

Search Engine Optimization

Of all the options for organic traffic growth, search engine optimization—also known as SEO—is probably the most powerful. This includes traffic from both search engines, such as Google, as well as traffic from Pinterest, which many people often mistake for social media, but is actually considered a visual search engine.

Because search engine traffic is such an important strategy, we're going to take a deeper dive in the next chapter, but for now you should know this—SEO isn't as technical or complicated or as hard to master as it might sound. It's really just about including the right data on your website and blog posts to allow your content to be indexed and found.

Social Media

Unless you've been living under a rock, you are probably at least somewhat familiar with the various options for social media—Facebook, Twitter, Instagram, LinkedIn, Tumblr, YouTube, Reddit, SnapChat, etc. the list goes on and on.

And I don't know about you, but I sometimes look at that list and immediately feel stressed out. How is anyone supposed to keep up with all that social media and still build a sustainable business?

Here's my highly subjective short answer: You're not. Most social media is a complete waste of time, especially when you are spreading yourself so thin that you can't actually get traction anywhere.

If you are treating your blog like a business—which you should be—then your social media time should always be viewed in terms of Return on Investment (ROI). The return, of course, is the number of social media followers you are able to convert into email subscribers and customers. Having a million Twitter followers is great, but if almost none of them actually turn into raving fans who know, like, and trust you, what is the point?

The biggest problem with most social media platforms these days is that trying to build them is an uphill battle. The algorithms are not working in your favor. And that means that you can spend a ton of time trying to build engagement and get more followers, but your progress will probably be painfully slow, and for what? So that you can show off those vanity metrics and tell people how popular you are?

I'd rather see you be profitable than popular. And that means that in terms of organic growth strategies, I'm not actually a big fan of social media, just for the sake of being on social media. I think more often than not, it becomes a distraction rather than a tool to grow. Instead, when it comes to growing your business, I'd recommend focusing your time and energy on activities that can produce predictable results.

Of course, that's also where our paid growth strategies come into play.

PAID GROWTH STRATEGIES

When your online business is still brand new and not yet generating any sort of income, it can be pretty scary to start thinking about investing real dollars into promoting a business that is still unproven. And yet, if you want to be able to grow your business faster and more predictably, paid growth strategies are generally the way to go.

Most paid growth strategies involve paid advertising—either on a platform like Facebook, Pinterest, or Google, or possibly even paying another business or brand to promote your own.

The only real way to know which one is the best platform for your business and products is to invest some money into testing to see which one is getting results.

We'll be diving into exactly where you should start with this in the next chapter, but for now you should know that in order to make paid growth strategies a viable option and worth the investment, you're going to need to have some sort of product to sell.

In the meantime, you should also know what kind of paid growth strategies you should **avoid at all costs**. These include questionable practices, such as paying to buy followers on social media, buying email subscribers (unless you're buying an existing business with an already established list), and black hat SEO. None of these options will help you build a legitimate business, and in many cases, they can even hurt your business. So just don't do it.

Chapter 4 Action Plan: Start Getting Found

- ❏ Start telling people about your blog and asking them to read it—your friends, family members, neighbors, etc. Have business cards printed and get into the habit of sharing your elevator pitch.
- ❏ Comment regularly on other blogs and websites in your niche.
- ❏ Network and collaborate with other entrepreneurs and online business owners by joining online groups or attending conferences or local meet-ups.
- ❏ Submit guest-post inquiries to several larger websites within your same niche.

chapter 5

Growth Strategies Worth Focusing On

"There's so much to do. How do I know the things I'm spending time on are the things that will actually make an impact on my business and help me grow?"

It's a question I hear almost every week from my students at Elite Blog Academy. Many of them feel paralyzed by the fact that there are so many different options for growth, so many different social media platforms they "should" be participating on, so many things to do all the time, and seemingly never enough time to do any of them really well.

It's very easy to get so caught up in doing "All. The. Things." that you never actually make any progress on any of them, but the truth is that focusing on just a few of the most effective strategies for growth—both paid and organic—will ultimately allow you to make the biggest impact in the shortest amount of time.

How much time?

Sorry friend, but this one is impossible to predict. For some of my EBA students, it happens fast, in just a few months, but that's usually because they're starting with some sort of existing platform or experience. For others, especially those who are brand new to content marketing, it takes a little longer, sometimes even a year or more.

And while I can't give you an exact time frame, I can tell you that for most content-marketing based businesses, the trajectory looks something like this:

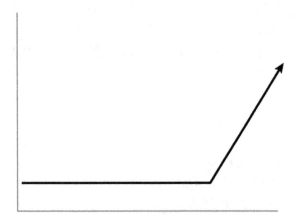

You work really hard for a while, refining your message, figuring out what you want to say, how you're going to say it, and exactly who you are saying it to. You focus on figuring out what most resonates, then putting it out there into the world, and sharing it in all the ways you know how. Basically, you throw a whole bunch of spaghetti against the wall, over and over again.

And then, one day, it happens.

Something sticks. A post you write really resonates, and it starts to get shared. And then you're able to do it again. And again. And suddenly what had been a flat line takes a sharp turn, and you start to gain a whole lot of momentum.

It's a trajectory I've watched happen over and over and over again; both in my own business, for thousands of Elite Blog Academy students, and one that will happen for you too if you're willing to push through the frustration that happens when it feels like you're not making much progress, even though in fact you actually are.

And while it's impossible to predict exactly how long it will take to start generating that real momentum in your business, I do believe there are some growth strategies that will help you get there a whole lot faster.

PUMP OUT GREAT CONTENT

The first time one of my blog posts went "viral", I felt like I had hit the traffic jackpot. I had been writing for more than two years, writing lots of posts that I was plenty proud of, including quite a few that generated a great response from the small but loyal readership I had worked so hard to grow.

Then one day I wrote a post about why I took all my kids' toys away (and why they wouldn't get them back), and something about what I wrote resonated. It struck a nerve and got people talking. Some readers were completely horrified. They told me I was a terrible mother who was scarring my children for life. They started hate groups, forum threads, and even threatened to call CPS. One person even started a Tumblr site dedicated to hating me.

But many more people were completely inspired by it. They wrote to tell me they had dreamed of doing the exact same thing, but had never dared. They shared how reading my story had given them the courage to make necessary changes, and how their kids and family were so much happier as a result.

And love it or hate it, people began sharing the post with others, who in turn shared it with even more people. It got picked up by major media outlets, including the Daily Mail, which then led it to be shared even more. And in the years since, that same post has gone viral again and again.

The thing is, in a moment of frustration as a mom of two small kids, I had NO idea when I wrote it that it would be THE post that completely changed the trajectory of my entire business.

It wasn't some brilliant strategic move. I couldn't have predicted it. I don't even know that I would have chosen all the attention on that particular topic, had I known how it would all play out. And yet, when I look back on it, I can see that all the work I had done up until that point is exactly what allowed that moment of virality to catapult my business to the next level.

You see, by the time that post went viral, I had already been blogging for more than two years. And those two years were spent learning all the critical elements it takes to create consistently excellent content. By the time I had my big viral moment, I had already created something worth sticking around for. Many people found me for the first time from that viral post, but they stayed because of everything else that was there. If I had gone viral in my first month, I don't think it would have had nearly the impact.

And so, in that sense, I'm grateful that it took two years for that first viral post to happen, even though at many points during those two years, I felt like nothing was happening fast enough. But I'm so grateful that by the time my business really started to grow, I was ready.

When it comes right down to it, organic traffic is completely transparent. You can't trick it. You can't pay for it. You can't force it. It is truly the purest form of growth because it is based solely on the simple idea that **if people like what you have to say, they will share it with others.**

So what does that mean? It means—and pay attention because this is important—**your content will NOT help you grow your traffic if it's not consistently stellar.** Stellar content comes with time and with practice and with diligence. It means honing your craft, writing regularly, improving your images, and presenting it all in a package that makes your message clear and easy to understand. Once you've learned how to do all that—once you've mastered the art of creating amazing, compelling, truly pin-worthy and outstanding content—capturing organic traffic is the easy part.

It also means that one of your primary strategies for growing your audience needs to include regularly posting new content. In the beginning, when you're just trying to get traction, this means pumping out as much quality content as you possibly can. It's not enough to post once a week and think you're going to get there. Because the more you put out, the more likely you'll be to hit upon something that really resonates.

And it's not enough to just post 3 times a week, or 5 times a week, or even more if you can. You also need to be paying attention to what's working and what's not. And when something seems to resonate a little bit more, or get more attention or more views than anything else you've done, you need to do more of it. You need to constantly analyze your results to see if you can find patterns. You need to start hypothesizing "what if" scenarios, then testing your hypothesis to see if you're right. You need to try different types of posts, and write posts that meet specific felt needs for your avatar. You need to write posts that will strike a nerve—posts that take a strong stance or talk about something controversial (just make sure it is a controversy that fits within your niche)! You need to make sure that every post has at least 2— but preferably 3 or 4—pin-worthy graphics, because you don't know which image will get more traction. You need to test different titles and work hard to add a little salaciousness to your headlines so that people actually want to click on them.

You need to keep throwing that spaghetti against the wall until something sticks.

So start pumping out great content, and keep pumping it out until you land on something that's working. Remember, that flat line will feel flat and long for a while, but if you keep at it, and keep doing all those things I just mentioned, there will be a moment, a turning point where it all starts taking off. And that's when growing your business really gets fun!

EBA CASE STUDY:
Talaat & Tai McNeely, *His & Her Money*

Talaat and Tai from His and Her Money have been blogging for about 5 years and help couples better manage their money. They are very transparent with their audience and bring them into their life and home to show them EXACTLY how they climbed their way out of debt.

They started their blog in August of 2014 and roughly 3 months later they heard about Elite Blog Academy. They were already followers of Living Well Spending Less, and as they read through the course description, it outlined a bunch of things that they had been wondering about themselves. They had been a little apprehensive due to the cost, but now, credit EBA as the driving force that transformed their blog to a business.

EBA helped them create a strategy to magnify their message, refine their voice, and define the pillars of content they needed to stick to. This framework made them realize exactly how powerful it is to invest your time in the beginning on content. It is really the thing that helped them stay focused so they could be as impactful in their niche as possible. In their first year of blogging they made a total of $6,000. But in their second year, after joining Elite Blog Academy, they increased that income to $30,000!

They have continued to pump out amazing and relevant content that has continued to make an impact in their niche leading them to their wildly popular Podcast: His and Her Money Show.

OPTIMIZE FOR SEARCH RESULTS

The next growth strategy I recommend focusing on, if you truly want to maximize your efforts, is to make sure you are optimizing all that stellar content you are creating for search results on both Google and Pinterest. But when I say "next" strategy, please know that I don't mean "first work on content for a while, then work on optimizing for search results."

Instead, these strategies will be happening simultaneously. You'll need to be consistently pumping out stellar content AND continually optimizing that stellar content for both search engine and Pinterest traffic. You'll also want to make sure that you are specifically creating keyword-rich content that will help drive those search results. What solutions is your avatar looking for? Those are the things you'll want to write about.

So let's take a minute to talk about both SEO and Pinterest specifically, and a few things that you can do to optimize your content for good search results on both.

Search Engine Optimization

While the rise of "influencers" has kept a lot of attention on Instagram and YouTube, the reality is that search traffic can and should still be an important source of traffic for your online business. Search engine traffic tends to be the highly targeted type of traffic that is looking for solutions to a specific question or problem, which means that they tend to stay longer and are more likely to opt-in once on your site.

Since first starting my online business in 2010, I have spent a lot of time learning the ins and outs of SEO, reading pretty much every book and article I could get my hands on. If you really wanted all the boring details, I could probably talk your ear off for hours. Truthfully, if I thought knowing more boring details about the intricacies of search engine optimization would help you make more money, I would include it, but at the end of the day, I honestly believe that the only thing you really need to know about Google and SEO is this:

Google's ONLY goal is to bring the BEST possible results for a given search.

This means that you can't trick Google into thinking you've written the best post ever about how to catch a dragonfly if your post is actually about how to catch grasshoppers. The Google algorithms are incredibly sophisticated, looking at everything from the content itself to how long visitors that are searching for a particular topic stay on that page.

SEO is not about "tricking" Google, and you should be extremely wary of any service that promises they can. SEO is really more about helping Google understand what your post is *actually* about, rather than figuring out the hottest search term. You do this by adding title tags, meta descriptions, and meta keywords, which sounds much more complicated than it actually is. Here's a brief overview:

Title Tag: The title tag refers to the words that show up at the very top of your browser window when you open a particular web page. The default title tag is generally the post title, but you can change the title tag to be whatever you want it to be. The title tag is also what shows up in bold in the Google search results. It can be as long as you want it to be, but Google will only read and use the first 70 characters, so it is generally best to keep it to 70 characters or less. Of the three on-site optimization choices, I have found the title tag to be the most important and the most relevant to Google. Thus, at the bare minimum, you should ALWAYS take the time to optimize your title tag.

Meta Description: The meta description helps tell Google what your post is about, and it is also what shows up underneath the bold title in your Google search results. I have found it helpful for "selling" a particular post that is already getting good search results, but not always absolutely necessary. The default meta description, if you leave this field blank, is the first 150 words of your post.

Meta Keywords: Meta keywords are any search keywords or phrases you would like to see associated with your post. Google doesn't give much weight to meta keywords, but other search engines, such as Yahoo and Bing, do consider meta keywords in their results, which makes this field worth filling out as well.

For Wordpress, there are a variety of SEO plug-ins, such as Yoast, that allow you to customize your metadata for each post.

Here are a few examples of how I optimize my posts:

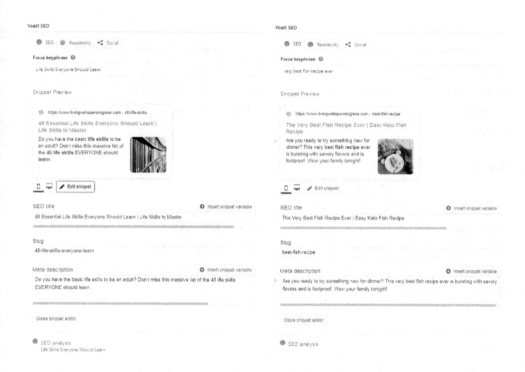

One strategy I do recommend when it comes to SEO is optimizing your pages—your title tags in particular—for more specific long-tailed keywords. Simply put, a long-tail keyword is a string of keywords such as: "how to make a paper party hat," rather than just "party hat." Remember, Google's goal is to match the best results to a particular search, so you are better off showing up as the top post to the 100 people who are searching for "how to make a paper party hat" than as the 100th result to the 100,000 people who are searching for "party hat."

Links are also important when it comes to SEO—both the outside links that come to your site from other websites, as well as the way that you interlink your posts to one another. I recommend interlinking your posts as much as possible, and when doing so, make sure that you are hyperlinking keywords, (as opposed to common words such as "here"). Those links help confirm to Google exactly what your post is about. And one easy way to get links from other sites is to leave comments and include your URL. (Just make sure they are actually genuine and helpful comments so you don't get deleted as spam!)

Remember also that quality content counts for a whole lot—at least as much as all the on-site optimization you can do—and if Google sees your site as spam, with too many posts, too much duplicate content, or too many very short posts, you will get majorly penalized. These days, posts over 1,000 words tend to get the best traction with SEO.

Pinterest

Not too long ago, Pinterest was the traffic secret of bloggers and online business owners everywhere. All you had to do was get added to a few group boards and then start sharing your posts regularly on this almost magical platform and you could be guaranteed a steady stream of page views coming your way. In fact, a large portion of the previous edition of this book was dedicated to highlighting all the wonders of Pinterest.

And then, like other social sharing sites before it, things started to change. In the interest of preserving user experience, Pinterest began cracking down on—and even penalizing—what it saw as "spam", which was really just too much pinning of the same content, especially content that wasn't all that good. The algorithms, which had previously presented all the content in chronological order, began focusing on delivering the content that was most popular or related to what people were actually searching for.

This was good news for Pinterest users, but a hard pill to swallow for all online business owners who had come to expect and rely on that steady stream of free traffic. Many were outraged and indignant, forgetting that Pinterest's primary interest and responsibility was not in helping bloggers get free traffic, but in creating a user experience that makes their users keep coming back.

So why am I telling you this?

Because I think it highlights an important point that is easy to forget when things are going well or something is coming easy—that when it comes to your business, you don't get to control what other people or businesses do. And so, if you decide to build your entire business or platform on the back of someone else's business or platform, you are leaving yourself wide open to destruction in the event they decide to change something—*which they will.*

If you want to have a business that is sustainable and predictable for the long term, then you need to abandon the belief (a belief that is all-too common in many blogger and influencer circles) that your traffic should come cheap and easy. No one owes you anything. Not Facebook, not Pinterest, not Google, not Instagram. Your job is to figure out how to create predictable traffic and revenue in your business, and to focus on growing the thing you do have control over—your email list.

We're going to talk more about paid traffic in just a minute, and all about how and why to grow and leverage your email list in the next chapter. But for now, I want to bring us back to Pinterest. Because while Pinterest is no longer the "magical" source of free traffic it was a few years ago, it is still a very important tool for online business owners, and when it comes to the best strategies for growing your business, it is still a tool worth putting some time and effort into.

You see, over the past few years, Pinterest has slowly transformed itself from a social media platform, which was based on followers and social interaction, to a visual search engine—a place where users can come to search for ideas.

Knowing this, you should approach optimizing for Pinterest in much of the same way you approach optimizing for search results on Google. Basically, this means renaming your photos to be something other than "DSC4589" and instead using searchable keywords in the photo title and description, as the photo description and title play a big role in influencing search results on Pinterest. This is something that only takes a minute to do for each photo, but can really make a big impact—not necessarily immediately, but definitely over time.

Like with Google, Pinterest can sometimes feel a little frustrating because things don't always happen fast, but the benefit of playing the long game here is that the little bit of effort you put in now can help drive traffic and get you results for years to come.

EBA Case Study:
Cristina Nivini, No Time for Style

Cristina Nivini is one of our amazing international students. She is a fashion blogger at No Time for Style and currently lives in Europe. When she began EBA, she already had a blog and had even made good progress in some areas. She already published a signicant amount of valuable content, but what she did not have was structure or a strategy. Cristina was confident she could get that from Elite Blog Academy.

And boy did she catch the EBA bug fast! She found that working through the assignments became a slight obsession of hers—igniting a passionate spark for her blog she didn't entirely expect. You see, when Cristina first started her blog, she really intended for it to be a side hobby from the main translating business she had already been running. She had run this business for several years, while also being a mom, and knew it was time to carve out a creative space for herself. But as an economist, she couldn't ignore the entrepreneurial spirit.

Cristina very quickly recognized the power of understanding where your people live, and spent her time and focus there. For herself, as a fashion blogger, her people were on Pinterest. She spent her time trying different things on Pinterest; figuring out what was working and what wasn't working. It is also important to note that Cristina works even harder because she blogs in multiple languages, which means that anytime she creates a new graphic for Pinterest, she takes the time to create an eye-catching graphic several times for each language. And it has paid off. Furthermore, because she spent her time and focus on this one social media platform instead of trying to do them all at once, she saw incredible results! She was getting 100,000 pageviews a month as a fairly new blogger.

But here is the thing, taking EBA incredibly serious, Cristina took it a step further. She knew that while she was doing something right on Pinterest (because it was the source of 97% of her traffic), it was not enough. While she was celebrating these visitors to her site as a win, she needed a plan for them. She realized it was time to work on her mailing list so she could begin capturing those leads, not only on Pinterest, but on her own platform as well.

Her email list is something she owns. And because she took that step, she was able to successfully launch her first product (which she notes was completely foreign and at times an overwhelming process for her). BUT with the steps laid out for her by EBA, she did it! AND not only that, she is now launching her second product!

We love Cristina's story for a few reasons: 1) We love the success that she is having blogging not only outside of US but also blogging in another language, and 2) we love how her journey perfectly demonstrates the need to focus on where your people are, but have a plan in place for them when they get there. EBA gave Cristina the steps that she needed to structure and refine her content, grow her audience, and ultimately monetize her business, which presented her with the new challenges she had been craving in her life.

USE PAID PROMOTIONS

When you're trying to get your online business off the ground—and especially when you're on a tight budget—the idea of investing hundreds or thousands of dollars into paid advertising can feel pretty daunting. After all, no one wants to just throw their money away on a strategy that may or may not work, when it seems like there are just as many FREE strategies for growing your audience that may or may not work.

But if you want to grow faster, and if you want to maintain a measure of control and predictability over your online business, then you really do need to incorporate paid promotions into your strategy, whether it be on Facebook, Pinterest, or Google.

Of course, in developing your paid advertising strategy, it is essential to first look at your objectives. What is it that you want to accomplish? Is your goal to drive traffic, drive leads, or drive sales? Are you most interested in growing your audience for future income, or are you actually trying to sell a product right now? Do you simply want to get people to your website or do you have a specific purpose, such as building your email list?

If your goal is simply to grow your traffic or get people on your website, you will probably find that paying for promotion is a losing proposition, and you will probably not see enough of a return to make your investment worthwhile. In that case, you're better off focusing your time and effort on creating the best quality content that you possibly can, and then driving traffic through the organic strategies we've already talked about.

On the other hand, if your goal is to grow your email list, sell a product, or both (which it should be, by the way), then paid advertising is definitely well worth your investment.

So before you actually set up your first ad, let's talk about a few things you'll want to think about before you head down this path.

What's your hook?

If you want to use paid advertising to grow your email list, you'll need something to promote in order to attract subscribers. This is known as a lead magnet, but is also sometimes called a "freebie," "subscriber incentive," "free download," or "free printable." Whatever you decide to call it, you'll need at least one (and possibly many more). We'll be talking about these more in the next chapter, but in the meantime, know that you'll want to come up with something free to give away that is very targeted to your specific avatar's biggest felt need.

Here is an example of a lead magnet promotion that we run on Living Well Spending Less:

What are you selling?

Paid advertising makes a whole lot more sense when you're using it to drive sales. And that means that before you start investing a ton of money into ads, you'll also want to create some sort of digital product that you can offer to anyone who opts in for your freebie (often called a "tripwire" or an "upsell"), and that you can sell on its own. This first product should be something you can create relatively quickly, and again, it should be very targeted to your specific avatar's biggest felt need, and it should offer a significant upgrade to whatever you're giving away for free.

Here are some examples of the digital products that we sell in this way at Living Well Spending Less:

Where are you sending people?

A lot of online business owners, when running their first ads, make the mistake of thinking that you should be sending people to the website that you've just worked so hard to create. But that's actually not true. In order to get the best conversions possible, you'll want to direct your ads to a specific landing page—also known as a Lead Page—in order to make sure there is only one call-to-action (CTA) on that page.

CREATE A LIFE YOU LOVE WITH THE
SANITY-SAVING LIVING WELL PLANNER®

How will you pull it all together?

To make your ads work, you'll need to think through how all these different elements will work together. This is called creating your sales funnel, and for online business owners, putting together a sales funnel that actually converts and drives both leads and revenue for your business is pretty essential. Over time, your sales funnel might get longer and more complex, with more products added to it. But to start, your simple sales funnel might look something like this:

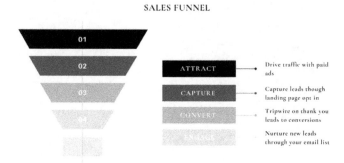

Paid Ad → Opt In Page → Thank You Page (Tripwire) → Email List

For more guidance in setting up your first simple sales funnel and your first paid promotion, please check out our free training video at **EliteBlogAcademy.com/firstfunnel**.

Chapter 5 Action Plan: Focus on the Growth Strategies That Will Have the Biggest Impact

- ❏ Create consistently excellent content; dare to be polarizing and controversial, and make sure your post titles are designed to grab people's attention and get people to click.
- ❏ Consistently optimize your website, content, and images for search engine results on both Google and Pinterest.
- ❏ Strategically re-pin your best pins on a regular basis & take advantage of sharing & scheduling platforms such as Tailwind to allow your content to be seen by others.
- ❏ Strategically utilize paid advertising to grow your audience, particularly your email list, and set up your first simple sales funnel.

Chapter 6

Your Most Powerful Weapon

"How much of your time are you spending working on specifically growing and nurturing your email list?"

This was the question I asked at a recent event, when I conducted an impromptu survey of the 500 or so online business owners in the room. I quickly discovered that nearly everyone in the room was spending less than 5% of their time in that area. Most were spending less than 1%, and only a very small handful were spending even 10%.

For most online business owners, email just isn't a big priority.

But here's the thing—if I have been convinced of anything since writing the first edition of this book way back in 2013, it is of the superiority of focusing on your email list versus all other methods of traffic growth. Quite frankly, it blows everything else out of the water.

Even so—and this never ceases to amaze me—most bloggers and influencers just refuse to give it the attention it deserves.

And honestly, I get it, I really do. When it comes to blogging and growing an online business, email is one of those things that never feels like a priority, and so we constantly push it to the back burner in favor of all the other things that FEEL so much more important, things like getting that next blog post up, and promoting it on social media, and responding to all those emails and blog comments, and interacting on Facebook… all the daily hustle that makes you feel like you've accomplished something important, when in fact, you probably haven't.

It's so hard to put off what feels important RIGHT NOW for what will be important in the long term. We're all guilty of getting sucked into the tyranny of the urgent.

But the reality is that the only way to break free of all that hustle, and instead create an audience of loyal, dedicated fans and create a sustainable, long term business, is to spend more time on building your foundation.

You have to play the long game, not the right now game.

And taking the time to grow and nurture your email list is playing the long game.

I truly can't emphasize this point enough—whether you call yourself a blogger, podcaster, influencer, author, or online business owner, email is, hands down, your most powerful weapon. And that means that if you aren't continually focused on growing and nurturing your list, you are going to be stuck in the land of endless hustle.

Just consider these facts about email marketing.

First, email's return on investment is massive. For every $1 you spend on email marketing, your businesses can expect a $38 return[6]. Second, when it comes to interacting, people are twice as likely to sign up for your email list as they are to engage with you on social media. Third, contrary to popular belief (or online business owner paranoia) most people are not sick of email! 61% of consumers say that they actually enjoy receiving promotional emails when those emails are personalized. 38% say they would actually like to receive MORE emails. Fourth, email is the best way to reach a mobile audience. 88% of mobile users check their email on their phone, which makes email more popular than any other app. And finally, email converts your readers into paying customers, that's 40% higher than all social media channels and search engines COMBINED.

I don't know about you, but to me, those are some pretty compelling reasons to spend more time working on growing and nurturing your email list!

But I'll give you a few more, straight from my own experience.

First, your email list is yours. No one else can take it away from you. You have complete control. You don't get that anywhere else! Your blog is dependent on page views, and if something happens—say Google, Facebook, or Pinterest changes their algorithms and suddenly your traffic drops—you will be in big trouble.

With email, you have complete control. It's yours.

In my own business, I've seen this firsthand, having more than doubled our revenue every year since 2014; despite the fact that my blog's page views are less than half of what they were in 2014. Although my page views have dropped, my email subscribers keep climbing—to over a million subscribers at last count.

But more importantly—at least to me—is the fact that your email subscribers are far more likely to be YOUR PEOPLE than anyone else on the Internet. They are your tribe. Pinterest can be a nice way to get traffic, but let me tell you, those are not your people. I guarantee at least half the people who come to your site via Pinterest don't even know they're not on Pinterest anymore, or that yours is a separate site.

Facebook and Instagram are a nice way to say hi, but for the most part, those aren't really your people either. You are just one more voice in a very crowded room. The way I look at it, the people you interact with on Facebook or Instagram are sort-of like that neighbor down the street that you don't really know, but you always wave to as you are driving by.

Oh sure, you're friendly enough, in the most casual way possible, but you don't have a relationship.

Email, on the other hand, is your chance to create that relationship. Those are the neighbors you invite in for a cup of coffee. Those are the neighbors who know you and trust you, and actually want to listen to what you have to say and take your advice. Those are your raving fans.

If you truly want to build a successful and sustainable online business through your blog or website, then email is where it is at. It is, hands down, your MOST powerful weapon as a blogger. You need to use it well.

Of course, that brings us to the big question, doesn't it?

HOW?

How do we grow and nurture our list in order to create a tribe of raving fans?

Now just a side note—before you start building your list, you'll want to make sure you have chosen an email provider that can grow with you. There are lots and lots of options to choose from, and you can find our most up-to-date recommendations at eliteblogacademy.com/resources.

But in the meantime, now that I've hopefully convinced you just how vitally important this unit is to your long-term success, let's spend some time reviewing...

EBA Case Study:
Heidi Vilegas, *Healing Harvest Homestead*

Heidi, of Healing Harvest Homestead, was depressed and frustrated with her job as a teacher. She loved teaching and she adored her students, but she was so fed up with the testing requirements, the institution, and the fact that her job as a teacher had changed so much. She knew something had to change.

She had started a blog as an outlet, but when she felt the urge to leave her job and get serious about blogging, she knew she needed some help, and begged her husband to let her join EBA. Once she did, her blog has continued to grow ever since. She started out with no email list, but EBA taught her how to set that up and get the ball rolling. Once she did, Heidi discovered very quickly why and how an email list is an ESSENTIAL part of growing a business.

Her first goal was to make $1,000 a month. After talking with her husband, together they decided that if she could earn $2,000 a month, she could retire early. That was all she needed to hear to supercharge her motivation.

Not only did she reach that mark, but she reached it 5 YEARS EARLY. Heidi was able to retire 5 years earlier than planned because of her blog and EBA. But not only that, she is now earning MORE income on her blog than her retirement income. As a retired teacher who loves teaching, blogging has given Heidi a way to use her gifts to not only help those sitting in her classroom, but a platform to teach thousands and create the life she's always dreamed of with her family.

MAKE EMAIL YOUR TOP PRIORITY

Our first strategy is to simply to make email your top priority. You've got to be completely single-minded when it comes to email!

And while this might not even seem like a strategy, it is actually probably the most important strategy of all, and if you can implement and embrace this strategy, you will ultimately win.

As a blogger or online business owner, you need to always, always, always make email your top priority. It has to come first, before writing blog posts or tweaking your site design, or taking another course, or chatting in a Facebook group. It is far too easy to get distracted by all the other "stuff" that's out there, calling for your attention, and it is far too easy to put growing and nurturing your email list constantly on the back burner, because it just doesn't FEEL important.

That means that you need to figure out a way to make email FEEL important, even if it means putting a giant sign above your desk that says "GROWING AND NURTURING MY LIST IS MY TOP PRIORITY."

It means that you need to be intentional about blocking out time each week for writing your emails and for focusing on your list growth strategy. It means you need to get intentional about A-B split testing and creating Lead Magnets and learning how to master Facebook ads and adding opt-in boxes to every blog post.

It means that you will need to make email growth, not page views or engagement, the focus of your social media strategy. It means you will stop worrying about vanity metrics, and start measuring your success ONLY in the number of email signups you are adding on a daily basis.

And, perhaps most importantly, it means that you have to be willing to invest in growing your list, because believe me, it is probably the most important and valuable investment that you will make when it comes to your blog.

It means email will be your FIRST thought, not an afterthought.

For most online business owners, that's a big shift. And sadly, what I notice is that no matter how much I talk about how important email is for your business, way too many bloggers and online business owners get caught up in the idea that they need to focus on getting more page views from Pinterest, or growing their followers and getting more engagement on Instagram. So many online business owners just don't get it.

Don't let that be you.

What is it going to have to change in your day-to-day schedule for growing and nurturing your email list to go from 2% of your time to 20%, or from 10% to 40%? How all-in are you willing to be when it comes to email?

Because here's the thing you need to know—growing your list? It's not really that hard, and if you are frustrated that your list isn't growing, I would dare to guess it is because you haven't made it your top priority, or that you're not daring to invest in your business or in your list.

And I can tell you that on my team, email has been our top priority for a very long time. It is the sole focus of our social media strategy. Managing, growing, and nurturing our list is where we spend the bulk of our time, energy, and budget for our company, and where I personally spend a huge chunk of my own time as well. And all of that diligence pays off—we average almost 1000 new leads every single day.

If you are worried that this is hard, you're psyching yourself out. But to get that kind of growth, email can't be something that you do half-heartedly, or be something that you think about every once in a while. It is something you look at and work on DAILY. It has to mean that no matter how someone gets to your site—whether they come through an organic search, Pinterest, Facebook, or Instagram—you don't just wave and say hi, you invite them in for coffee again and again. You invite them to become part of your tribe.

Of course, once they're on your list, you make sure they want to stay there. And that brings me to strategy #2.

BE GENEROUS

You see, it's not enough to JUST focus on growing your list. You also need to make your list worth subscribing to! That means you have to give away something special in your emails, something that your subscribers can't get anywhere else.

If you happen to subscribe to my company via email, you probably already know that we send out a lot of content every single week that's not found anywhere else. Do we sometimes link to blog posts or our websites in those emails? Absolutely! But the content itself is new, fresh, and only available via email.

And you know what? The people who subscribe to our list, for the most part, LOVE getting those emails! Every year we do a reader survey, and every year, we discover that our emails are people's most favorite thing. And to be honest, the main reason our emails are so popular (I think), is because we work very hard to make sure that each and every week we are addressing our avatar's felt needs. What I write feels personal, and while I often share stories or examples from my own life, it is never actually about me. It is always about them.

Now, do we also have people who unsubscribe? Of course we do! Every single day! But that's okay, because those people are not our people. They are not our tribe. And we know that in order to attract the right people, you have to repel the wrong people. So we celebrate the unsubscribes!

If you've ever signed up for one of our lists, you probably also know that we give a TON of stuff away! We have a welcome sequence that starts by introducing ourselves and letting people know what to expect, and then we send out a series of free gifts just as thank you for being part of our community.

We also regularly send out coupons for free products in our shop, and invitations to free trainings and mini-courses. We try to make it a point to give more than we ask. Even when we are running a sales campaign, we try to make sure the content is valuable, interesting, and worth reading, regardless of whether someone purchases the product we are promoting. And I always know we are on the right track when we get thank you letters in response to a sales email!

Being generous is also the way to get your prospects to subscribe in the first place. You'll need to create some sort of subscriber incentive or lead magnet, like I briefly mentioned in the last chapter, which you'll give away in exchange for someone signing up to your email list. This can be pretty much anything, but I recommend not making your freebies too big or overwhelming. It should be something helpful and valuable that delivers a quick win.

Here are a few examples of successful lead magnets that we've used in our company:

From there, you'll need to make sure you are promoting your lead magnet, both on your website (in as many places as possible) as well as on social media. And then, once you have your first paid product to use as an upsell, you should be running ads to help grow your list as well. We'll talk a bit more about that in the next part of this book.

But for now, know that the secret to growing your list is generosity—be willing to give more than you ask!

EBA Case Study:
Tracy Lynn Shugerts, *Simple Living Country Gal*

Tracy Lynn Shugerts blogs at Simple Living Country Gal, where she writes about all things simple living. From goats to gardens, decluttering, and frugal tips, she helps folks learn how living simply can help them create a life they love. Her main reason for starting her business was so she could earn enough money to pay off her kids' student loan debt, so they could have less stress about what they owe.

Tracy joined our community back in 2016, and not only have we recognized her unique niche, but also her incredibly true talent for providing real and valuable content. We love her story because she helps demonstrate that, despite what you may read on the internet, you do not have to blog in a certain niche to build an online business.

She's also AMAZING at using her knowledge and the tools available to focus on her "most powerful weapon"—her email list. Every action she takes on her blog, (a social media post, a blog post, and especially on her lead magnets, etc.), has her email growth in mind.

Tracy understands just how instrumental giving away that value for free is in nurturing those new subscribers to her email list. When she began putting her attention on her email list every single day, is when things really began to change. First her list grew, and she was able to see what content was resonating with her readers. Then she took it a step further and followed up on the most popular blog posts. This simple action allowed her to get inside her readers heads, create a freebie that spoke to her readers felt need, and led to building trust with her audience.

A perfect example is a blog post she wrote about having a stress-free Thanksgiving. She knew what her readers were looking for when they landed on her post, so she created a lead magnet she knew they would need: A Thanksgiving Planner.

By taking the time to be intentional about the content she is providing, she is proving to her new subscribers that she not only understands them, but can help them! Then those new subscribers told her what they wanted, which she then created, and then in turn was able to sell to them. She has grown her email list to well over 10,000, it's still growing, and she is making a full-time income doing what she loves!

BE CONSISTENTLY INTERESTING

In Chapter 2 of this book, we talked about the importance of creating great content, along with some practical strategies of how to make sure you're content is resonating—do you remember what they were? Just in case that was too long ago, I'll sum it up in one simple sentence: DON'T BE BORING!

Well, the same holds true for the emails that you send to your list! Your emails should be something your readers look forward to opening, something that is always worth their time.

For the record, an auto-generated RSS feed of your latest blog posts is not that interesting. But a funny story that makes people chuckle and also makes a great point? That's interesting. A stale, unimaginative sales pitch or generic swipe copy? Not that interesting. A helpful tip that addresses a felt need and that also happens to promote a product that addresses the same felt need? That's interesting!

The key to building a great relationship with your list and growing a loyal tribe of raving fans is not JUST to be interesting once in a while, it is to be consistently interesting. It starts from the moment they subscribe. Let your subscribers know what they can expect from being part of your list. Let them know how often you'll be contacting them, and what sort of benefit they will receive from being part of your community.

Then, and this is the important part—deliver on that promise! Be consistent with the quality and schedule of emails that you send out. Deliver consistent excellent content on a regular basis. Become a fixture in your subscriber's lives. Keep building that relationship so that they begin to know, like, and trust you, and really look forward to hearing from you.

It's the relationship that your business will be built on, and it is worth doing right.

Chapter 6 Action Plan: Leverage the most powerful weapon in your business

- ❑ Commit to making email your top priority when it comes to growing your audience. Don't be fooled by vanity metrics like page views or Instagram likes. The money is in your email list.
- ❑ Create at least one lead magnet to incentivize people to subscribe to your list.
- ❑ Create a strong welcome sequence and create email content that is generous and consistently interesting.

PHASE 3 | MONETIZE

Once you're clear about who you're talking to and what you're going to say, and then once you've seen that message start to resonate and your audience start to grow, your next move is to start focusing on monetization. Because remember—if you want to have a business, you're going have to start selling something.

But know this--just because you start selling, doesn't mean you'll stop refining and growing. Those things will always be part of your business, which is why it is important not to get stuck in the refining or growing stages. Keep moving forward, and keep improving as you go.

In this section, we're going to start by all the different paths for monetization that you'll want to consider, as well as some of the pros and cons of each one. From there, we'll talk about why you'll need to start working on your products as soon as possible, and what that actually looks like. And then finally, we'll talk about the one secret to maximizing your revenue that every business owner needs to understand—that you've gotta make the ask, again and again and again. By the end of this section, you'll be ready to start driving revenue in a big way!

chapter 7

Show Me the Money

"Yes, I get that you have a website, and that people like to read it, and that you're very popular, but how do you actually make money?"

I first started my business in 2010. In the time since, I've written six bestselling books, have been featured in dozens of national magazines and appeared on national television more than once. My websites have received tens of millions of visitors, my podcast consistently ranks in the top 500 of all podcasts on the planet, I've got hundreds of thousands of followers on social media, and over one million email subscribers at last count. I've even given a TED talk.

And yet, at least once or twice a month, someone will ask me that question—*how do you actually make money?*

Even my family doesn't seem to understand what it is that I do for a living. In fact, I'm pretty sure that my parents still believe that we're surviving off of my husband's retirement, and that this cute little "blog thing" of mine is a very nice hobby.

It always makes me laugh, though, because the answer to how I make money is not some big mystery. There's no voodoo going on. It's not magic. I make money the same way every other business on the planet makes money—*by selling things.*

And all those numbers I just mentioned—the tens of millions of visitors and podcast downloads, social media followers and email subscribers—those numbers, while perhaps impressive, don't actually make me any money. At least not by themselves. Those numbers only actually mean something if I am also *selling* something. Otherwise they're just vanity metrics.

Because the honest truth is that I don't actually care about being popular, and you shouldn't either. I'm not interested in being famous. I don't want people to stop me in the street or ask for my autograph. I would actually much rather *not* be recognized. At heart, I'm an introvert, and the handful of times it has happened, it has been so incredibly awkward that I almost wanted to die.

But I digress.

Because, you see, what I actually care about is being *profitable.* After all, the name of this book is *How to Blog for Profit*, not *How to Blog for Popularity* (or *Page Views* or *Publicity* for that matter!)

Which brings me back to needing to *sell* things.

And in my company, we sell a *lot* of different things. This book for one, along with lots of other books and workbooks. We sell several different courses and resources on a variety of topics. We have a physical planner that we manufacture and sell. We also sell ad space on our website, and earn a commission on selling other people's products (something called affiliate marketing). I sell my time and expertise through coaching and live events, and every once in a while we'll even sell the opportunity to be mentioned in a blog post or an email (something called direct sponsorship or private advertising).

One reason I've had a lot of success with all that selling is because I have a lot of people to sell to. This is not an accident. I've worked hard to grow a super-engaged audience of people who know, like, and trust me, using all the strategies we talked about in the first half of this book.

But the most *important* reason I have a lot of success with all that selling is because **I'm actually willing to sell**. I am not afraid to ask for the sale.. In the grand scheme of things, the numbers that make me "popular" don't matter very much; what *does* matter is the number of readers, social media followers, and email subscribers that I can actually convert into paying customers.

While all online businesses make money by selling *something*, very few make money in exactly the same way, through exactly the same streams of revenue, or the same combination of those streams. To be honest, the beauty of having an online business is in its versatility. Because if you've managed to grow an audience, there are nearly an infinite number of ways to monetize your platform.

That said, I think that it is important to understand right off the bat that not all revenue streams are created equal. And if you're smart, you'll figure out how to leverage whatever size audience you've managed to build with the most profitable revenue streams possible.

And so, for the remainder of this chapter, I'm going to first briefly explain each of the four main revenue streams available to online business owners, along with some of the basic pros and cons of each. From there, we'll talk about what that actually looks like in practice, and how you can know you're pursuing the revenue streams in your business that will ultimately produce the greatest ROI.

EBA Case Study:
Amira Ameruddin, *Little Mushroom Cap*

Amira is one of our very talented members that joined our community in 2017. She blogs over at Little Mushroom Cap providing her readers with in depth tutorials on quilting. She is also one of our alumni that blogs on the side while still working full-time, which is amazing! She continues to prove time and time again that blogging is not only totally doable, but also profitable!

At first, Amira did not totally love the idea of selling to people. And we get it, a lot of people feel that way in the beginning. But, she realized something. She is not going door to door selling something to anyone who will listen for the sake of making a sale. She has been focused on growing her community; a community that FOUND HER to find solutions they needed.

She realized that making the ask, and making a sale to her community is actually helping them. And she tells us that when that concept clicked, it changed the way she approached her business. But Amira has told us that this does not only apply to products that come from her own heart and time, she has applied this concept to ANY sale she makes, whether it be affiliate promotions from other companies on products that she LOVES, or her own printable designs. And she has seen incredible results.

She is consistently earning a part-time income from her blog while still working at her job and continuing to grow! And she isn't seeing these results because she is popular, has high pageviews, or millions of followers; she is seeing these results because she is paying attention to her audience, their felt needs, offering them what they need, and most importantly making that ask!

THE FOUR STREAMS OF REVENUE

Of course, as excited as I am to finally dive into the portion of this book that will explain how you're actually going to start earning real money in your online business, it's also vitally important for you to understand that until you've built the foundation for your success that happens in Stages 1 & 2, it's going to be really hard to monetize successfully.

And so, as much as you may want to start here, with the money, it is essential that you take the time to make sure your content and presentation are resonating, and that you have at least begun to establish a strong connection with a growing audience before you try to focus on monetization.

And if you find that your income isn't what you want it to be, it probably means you will need to go back and work on refining your message and growing your audience some more in order to find the success that you are looking for.

When it comes to monetizing a blog, there are really only four main income streams to consider. Now keep in mind that this doesn't mean there are only four ways to make money on a blog—that's not what I mean at all. Within each of these four main categories of monetization, there is an endless number of possibilities, but in the end, everything you do to make money will fall under one of these four main streams.

Profit Through Ad Networks

The first strategy is profit through ad networks. If you think of your blog as virtual real estate, then profit through ad networks is revenue generated from leasing out your space to ad networks such as Google AdSense, who then fill the space with ads from their clients. The more page views your site receives, or the more ads that are competing for space in your particular niche, the more valuable your real estate.

In its simplest form, it looks something like this:

Most online business owners these days, if they choose to display ads on their web-sites, work with an ad network management service such as MediaVine, Monumet-ric, or AdThrive. They help make sure that the highest-paying ads are always being served on your site, which results in a higher CPM (cost per thousand visitors).

The biggest benefit of ad network revenue is that it tends to be the easiest and most passive way to earn an income on a blog, especially if you're working with an ad management service—you really don't have to do anything except watch the money roll in.

And while that might sound *amazing*, there are a couple of big downsides to relying on ad network revenue as your main revenue stream (besides the obvious one that ads can be annoying and ugly). The first is that depending on your niche, CPMs can vary greatly. Some websites are able to achieve CPMs of $20 or more, while others are stuck getting CPMs of just $2 or $3. The other downside is that to make any significant amount of money from ad networks, you'll most likely need a high num-ber of page views. Because even with $20 CPMs, you'll need 50,000 visitors to earn $1,000. That's a lot. And at the end of the day, if you have 50,000 visitors coming to your site every month, you should be making more than $1000.

This is not to say that ads are bad, or that you shouldn't have them on your website. If you are receiving a fair amount of traffic, they can be a nice way to supplement your revenue without adding any additional work to what you're already doing. These days, most people are so used to seeing ads on websites that they don't think anything of it. Just be careful not to make this your main goal, or your main source of revenue.

You *can* do better. I promise.

Profit Through Private Advertising

The second main monetization strategy available to online business owners is profit through private advertising and working directly with brands. This means selling ad space on your blog directly to a company or brand (and not through an ad network), or perhaps promoting a company in some other way on your website or social media channels, such as with a sponsored post or brand ambassadorship.

For some online business owners, especially those in the home design, DIY, food, or fashion niches, this can be an incredibly lucrative strategy. Many brands are eager to work with influencers and take advantage of the trust and rapport you've developed with your audience.

If you plan to work with brands, you'll want to take some time to put together a media kit and develop your own brand strategy. (For help with this, go to https:// eliteblogacademy.com/design-your-blog.) Once you have that done, you'll be ready to begin approaching brands and building relationships with potential advertisers, a process that sounds much scarier than it really is.

So where do you find brands to work with?

Well, pretty much everywhere! Many bloggers and online business owners use social-media agencies such as Clever Girls, Pollinate, Social Spark, and Yoked, just to name a few. The campaigns offered through this type of social-media agency are generally quite specific and well-defined, usually requiring their members to apply to be considered for a particular campaign. These campaigns, while easier to find, don't generally pay very well.

Your alternative to using an agency is to negotiate directly with brands that you meet on your own. You can do this by attending major blog conferences where you know there will be a lot of brands and sponsors in attendance. You can also send out direct unsolicited pitches to the companies that you'd most like to work with.

An example of an unsolicited pitch might look something like this:

Dear [name],

My name is [your name], and I operate a [description of your business] website called [name of website], which currently receives over [your number] unique visitors per month. I am a huge fan of [the product], and I would love to partner with your company to [brief description of what you'd like to do]. I'd love to set up a time to chat more about it if you are interested. Is there a time that works best for you?
Thanks so much,

[your name]

The downside of private advertising is that it can be time-consuming and frustrating. You have to be willing to deal with rejection, and willing to negotiate hard in order to get paid what you're actually worth. Often times—but not always—that energy could be better spent on creating and promoting your own products.

Profit Through Affiliate Revenue

The third monetization strategy is profit through affiliate advertising. This means using special tracking links to recommend products to your readers that other people own, then earning a commission when someone purchases those products.

This can be a very effective strategy for monetization, especially when you can find a product to promote that is both a good fit for your audience, and pays a high commission rate. Common sense would indicate that the more traffic a site receives, the more income it will earn through affiliate links, but surprisingly, this is not always the case.

From what I have observed, the most successful affiliate sales come from creating a relationship of trust with your readers. They will buy the things you recommend because they like what you have to say and they trust your opinion. I have seen bloggers and online business owners with relatively small audiences do extremely well with affiliate sales, simply because they have such an active and engaged audience who will happily buy almost any product they happen to talk about.

How well you do on affiliate sales on your site will depend somewhat on your niche—some genres clearly lend themselves to more sales than others—but also on how well you incorporate your own genuine interests and recommendations into your authentic content.

There are no shortage of affiliate networks and programs to choose from; these days almost every company selling a product offers some sort of affiliate program to entice online influencers to sell their products. Some are much better than others, so a big part of successful affiliate advertising means picking the networks with the most lucrative programs that are also a great fit for your particular business niche.

Probably the best-well known and most robust affiliate program out there, is the affiliate program offered through Amazon.com. And while the ease of use and fact that Amazon sells almost everything makes it a great program to join, the downside is that the payout for Amazon sales—ranging from 4–8.5 percent depending on how much you sell—is actually fairly low compared to many other affiliate programs. Thus, like with ad network revenue, if you want to make any significant amount of money through Amazon affiliate sales, you'll probably need to have a pretty big audience.

Even so, affiliate sales through Amazon can be incredibly lucrative for several reasons. First, almost anyone who shops online is already familiar with Amazon, has shopped there before, and has an account set up and ready to go. Second, Amazon's user-friendly affiliate interface allows you to deep-link—link directly to any page, category, or product on their site—which gives you the opportunity to easily link to any product you just happen to be mentioning in a given post. Third, Amazon's 24-hour cookies (as well as the fact that they sell everything under the sun) means that someone could feasibly click a link through your site for a book you recommend and end up buying a $600 bathtub. (And yes, that has actually happened to me!)

The main benefits of being an affiliate, versus selling your own products, are that, first of all, there is basically zero risk. As an affiliate for someone else's product, you don't have to assume any of the risk. There are no upfront costs in developing the product, and, if you don't manage to sell very many, you are only out a little bit of time. Another benefit of being an affiliate is that once you've made your sale and earned your commission, your work is done! Someone else gets to handle all that pesky customer service and product delivery. And third, you get to keep your entire commission. Every sale you make is pure profit, since you haven't invested anything into product development. What you sell is what you earn, plain and simple.

That said, if you want to successfully earn a sustainable revenue as an affiliate, you'll need to look beyond Amazon at other affiliate programs that offer much higher commissions, such as digital products and programs developed by other online business owners. These tend to pay much better (40-50% versus 4-6%), and are a much faster and easier way to generate a significant amount of revenue.

Profit Through Selling Your Own Product or Service

The fourth monetization strategy, which—I'm not gonna lie—is my unabashed personal favorite, is profit through selling a product. Your product could be anything from a book to an ebook, an online course to a service, or to an actual physical product that you manufacture and sell. There is usually a fair amount of work involved in creating & launching your product, but the payout is also usually much more significant.

One of the most game-changing moments in my business happened in 2014, when I attended a now-defunct conference called Launch. It was there that Dan Miller, of 48days.com, spoke the words that would change my business forever. He explained that his policy is that anytime readers ask the same question three times, he creates a product to fill that need.

This is genius! And if you can apply this policy to your business, I can almost guarantee that good things will start to happen.

The truth is that there are almost as many opportunities for making money from your talents or products as there are subjects to write about, and what's more, your readers are probably already asking for them!

What this means is that if you are interested in creating a product to sell, you need to *start by listening*. What are your readers and customers and prospective customers actually asking you for? What can't they get enough of? What are the questions you are answering over and over again? Figure it out and create a product that will *fill that need*.

It would be almost impossible for me to go into great detail about all of the products you can create, and I think it is important to note that your "product" is not always necessarily an object, but can also be your talent, service, or expertise. It could be coaching or consulting. It could be speaking. Really, truly, the sky's the limit.

So give yourself permission to start dreaming about all the possibilities.

EBA Case Study:
Amy Raines, *Deliberately Here*

Amy Raines is an EBA student that blogs at *Deliberately Here*, a homemaking blog that is geared towards busy moms who need quick tips and ideas to make their lives easier.

She wanted to start her online business so that she could make money while she stayed home to raise her family. After working on her business alongside Elite Blog Academy, that dream has become her reality. Her goal was to make $1,000 a month when she first started her blog, and exactly a year after working through EBA, she was making 6x that amount!

She very quickly learned the great power behind 1) focusing on her email list and 2) selling your own products. Ironically, these are two topics that bloggers tend to shy away from. Amy admits that a mailing list seemed highly unimportant as a new blogger, but that she always wished she had started her list sooner because the mailing list is where your business is—not in the pageviews.

You see, when you really tap into the power of content marketing and refine your message, your people will come to you which means you will already have an audience of raving fans practically telling you what products to create. And when you focus on your people, and providing them with what they need, that is when the magic happens. And that is exactly what students like Amy have done by following this framework. Now, selling her own products accounts for over half of her income! EBA gave her what she needed to turn her blog into her thriving online business.

AVOIDING THE DANGER ZONE

When it comes to successfully monetizing your blog, the goal is always to focus on the strategies that will generate the maximum revenue per reader. You want to make sure you are always leveraging the audience that you already have, rather than constantly trying to grow your audience in order to grow your revenue. Quite frankly, this is where a lot of bloggers and online business owners get stuck.

Because, when it comes to monetization, especially when you're just getting started, it's pretty easy to get frustrated. You look around and it seems like everybody and their DOG is making money on the Internet, and yet none of it seems to float your way. You're busting your butt trying to convince your friends and family to try to buy something off your Amazon link and wondering why the heck it has to be so hard!

And if that sounds like where you're at right now, then chances are, you've entered the DANGER ZONE.

You're working harder instead of smarter, focusing your attention on the wrong areas and selling yourself short. And unfortunately when it comes to blogging, there's not just ONE danger zone, there are many. Some of them we've already talked about—things like not knowing exactly who you are talking to, or being boring, or trying to spread yourself too thin.

But when it comes to making money online, there are three big income danger zones that you need to avoid at all costs. As we go over them, I want you to be really honest with yourself about your current strategy. Because if the money isn't rolling in the way you would like it to, chances are you are stuck in one of these three zones.

The good news is that identifying where you're getting stuck is the first step in breaking free.

Danger Zone #1: Playing the Page View Game

I'm pretty sure every blogger or online business owner goes through this phase at some point—checking your Google Analytics daily (sometimes even multiple times a day), obsessing over the numbers and willing to do anything just to get them a little bit higher.

The Page View Game constantly tells you that your revenue is wholly dependent on the number of page views that your site receives, which means that if you want to earn more money, you've got to keep increasing your traffic.

When you're stuck in the Page View Game, you're playing the short game. It's a daily struggle, one where the clock resets every night, and you have to start over yet again. It's like Groundhog Day. The same thing over and over again.

And let me tell you, If you want to spend your days as a blogger or online business owner completely and utterly exhausted by the hustle and on the fast track to burnout, then by all means, keep playing the Page View Game. Because when you make your income wholly dependent on the number of page views your blog receives, you become a slave. You are basically a crack addict, always needing that next fix.

You can't take the time to focus on big picture strategy, create real relationships, or generate long-term success because you are hopelessly dependent on getting that next big hit. And the saddest part of this strategy, besides being completely exhausting, is that it is not even very effective.

Let me quickly illustrate this with an example from my own business.

In 2013, the same year I wrote the first edition of this book, my business revenue was almost entirely dependent on ad networks. That was the year my business completely took off, and I averaged just over a million page views per month. That year, which was my first six-figure year as a blogger, about 75% of my revenue came from ad network revenue.

Do you know how much money I made per unique visitor to my blog?

$0.03.

Yep, that's right. A whopping THREE CENTS.

Now let's fast forward a few years.

Last year my business actually averaged less than a third of the page views it received in 2013, but my monetization strategy was completely different. This time ad networks only accounted for 1.1% of my total revenue. Product sales, on the other hand, accounted for 92% of our revenue.

And do you know how much money I made per unique visitor last year?

$1.26

In terms of revenue, that means I grew my business from the low six-figures to the high 7-figures. And if you are good at math, that means my business grew a whopping 4,100% in just five years. (And in case you're wondering, a 4,100% growth rate is insane.)

Please know that I'm not telling you this to brag. Because what I truly want you to understand from this example is that all this growth came from changing my monetization strategy, NOT from chasing page views.

It's really easy to get sucked into the Page View Game, because it seems like those numbers should matter more than they actually do. Believe me I know, because I was totally there, and I have seen a lot of bloggers get stuck there indefinitely. But it's a trap, and one you need to avoid at all costs.

Danger Zone #2: Bottom Feeding

Do you know what a bottom feeder is? A bottom feeder is a fish that fights over the scraps at the bottom, when there is a whole ocean full of giant fish just waiting to be caught.

Likewise, when it comes to the online business world, bottom feeders are the ones who are barely scraping by, fighting for the scraps and the tiny morsels, while ignoring the fact that there is a whole big ocean of opportunity out there.

And if you want to make money from your blog or online business—and I mean REAL money—you can't be a bottom feeder. You just can't. You are going to have to release yourself from that bottom feeder mentality, learn how to be a shark—or a killer whale instead.

So what are some of the warning signs that you might be a bottom feeder?

→ **You operate from a scarcity mentality**

A scarcity mindset says that there are not enough resources to go around. It is a zero-sum paradigm that makes you believe that there are limits on success, and that if someone else is successful, that will leave less room and less opportunity for you.

People who suffer from a scarcity mindset have a really hard time celebrating

145

other people's success, because in their mind, they believe that other people's success is taking away from their own. They can be overly competitive, jealous, and unwilling to share.

But when it comes to the internet—and life in general—scarcity is a big fat LIE! The internet is infinite, and your ability to make money is infinite as well. There is no shortage, and the fact that others are doing well is actually just proof of what's possible. Success begets success, and like ships in a harbor, we all rise together.

This is something we're going to talk about more in Chapter 10, but for now know that if you truly want to find success and make money, you'll need to replace your scarcity mindset with an abundance mindset.

→ You think everything is supposed to be free

Now don't get me wrong—I am all for getting a good deal wherever I can, not to mention all about giving away huge value to your readers. In my company, we give away lots of free content and resources on a regular basis, and that means there is probably a small portion of my audience that only ever takes advantage of the free stuff, and never actually pays for anything.

But that doesn't mean I'm afraid to charge for things.

Because the reality is that as humans, we value what we pay for. When you pay to invest in yourself, you'll value it more. And your readers are the same way. If you always give everything away for free, the message you are sending is that your content is not actually worth paying for.

→ You actually worry about low-paying affiliate links & freebies

Let's be honest—have you ever been irritated when a friend or family member made a big purchase on Amazon and didn't use your affiliate link? For a long time, I was the exact same way! It would drive me crazy that I was working my tail off, and they couldn't even be bothered to first click through my link.

Likewise, wasting your time and energy securing free products—often things you don't even need or want—and then having to write blog posts or share on social media is not a good use of your time.

It might seem like low hanging fruit, but the reality is that those kinds of activities are distracting you from making real money.

So stop wasting your time on the nickel and dime stuff.

Focus on the big picture.

Spend your time figuring out how to catch the big fish.

Danger Zone #3: Limiting Beliefs

In a nutshell, a limiting belief is a thought or belief we have about ourselves that holds us back from achieving our full potential. These limiting beliefs can come in all shapes and sizes, and appear in all different areas of our lives. They are also shape shifters—re-emerging in a new way each time we think we've overcome one.

And the reality is that we ALL have limiting beliefs about ourselves. Believe me, I've got plenty of my own, and I am constantly discovering more.

When it comes to blogging or starting a business, it might be that you don't believe that you actually have anything valuable to say, or that you aren't as talented, witty, or well-spoken as the blogger you admire most. It might be that you're not smart enough to be successful, that you don't want to invest in your blog or your business because you might fail. It might be that you don't want to reach out and ask for help because you might get rejected. It might be that you don't want to put 100 percent of your energy and effort into creating a successful business because you're not sure what the people around you will say.

Whether you are willing to admit it or not, there is probably a number floating in the back of your mind about how much you think you can make from your blog or online business.

"Oh I'd just be happy to make $100 a month from my blog."

"Maybe someday I'll be able to make $1000 a month."

"It would be so cool to make $5000 a month, but I don't think it will ever happen."

And chances are, you hear success stories about EBA students making $10,000, $20,000, $40,000 or even $100,000 a month and there is a little voice inside of you that says, "Oh sure, they did it, but I could never make that much."

THAT'S your limiting belief! That's the voice inside your head that puts a cap on what you are capable of.

But do you know what that voice is?

It's just a voice. It's just a thought, and nothing else.

While you can't always stop those limiting beliefs from popping up, you CAN refuse to listen to them. Because once you've recognized a limiting belief for what it is—just a thought that is holding you back—you can take away the power it has over you and move past it.

The reality is that the amount of money you can make online is infinite. There is an endless supply of money in the world, and there is nothing that says you can't have as much of it as you want.

It is only your limiting beliefs holding you back.

Chapter 7 Action Plan: Get Ready to Monetize

- ❏ Understand the four main strategies for earning money online, as well as the pros and cons of each.
- ❏ Start thinking about what strategies you might want to use in your online business.
- ❏ If you've already started monetizing your business, conduct an honest assessment of your current strategy to make sure that you are avoiding the three danger zones. Are you chasing page views? Bottom feeding? Getting caught up in your own limiting beliefs? What can you do to change that?

chapter 8

What Works (and What Doesn't)

_____

"I wish there were some way to know how, what I'm doing stacks up against what everyone else is doing. Is there something I could be doing better? How do I know whether I'm actually *winning*?"

I don't know about you, but I think for me, the hardest part of starting an online business was never quite knowing whether or not I was doing it *right*. Oh sure, if I Googled long and hard enough, I could find little nuggets of insight, into one particular topic or another, but there was no definitive set of instructions to follow, no guidelines or measurements to let me know whether I was on the right track, and no way to know the score.

All I really knew was how I was doing, and how much money I was making. So as long as it seemed like I was making pretty good money (as in, more than the $0 I had started with), and as long as my revenue kept going up, I figured I was doing okay.

In fact, if you had asked me in 2013 whether I thought I was winning, my answer would have been a resounding YES. I was generating a six-figure income! I had *millions* of page views! I thought I had *figured out* this whole blogging thing. In fact, I was so confident I wrote a book about it. And now, as I'm re-writing this 3rd edition, I find myself cringing at all the things I *thought* I knew. #howembarrassing

But as one of my EBA students recently told me, "sometimes you just don't know what you don't know until you know, you know?"

(Try saying that 5 times fast!)

So how does this relate to you making money?

Well, aside from being a really, *really* good lesson in humility, it's a good reminder that sometimes we can get so focused on one particular path or strategy that we sometimes just don't see that there might actually be a better way to do something. We believe that because we're seeing *some* success, or because something does seem to be working, that it's as good as it's going to get. As a result, we stop trying to improve.

But the truth is that we don't always know what's going to work until we try it, and even when something does work, there's a good chance it could be working better.

And instead of just telling you all of this, I thought it might be helpful to put my money where my mouth is and present you with some cold hard facts about what's working and what's not working when it comes to making money online.

For this, I decided to do an informal survey of online business owners who have turned blogging—or having an online business—into their full-time job.

Among other things, I wanted to find out whether there is, in fact, a connection between traffic and revenue. Is it true that more page views equals more revenue? Was my own experience an outlier? Or are there other online business owners who are crushing it with a smaller audience? I also wanted to find out what the most successful bloggers and online business owners are doing differently than everyone else. Where do they spend their time? What revenue streams are they focusing on? Finally, I wanted to know whether there is actually a definitive baseline for online business, be it a number or "score" that will tell you whether or not you are winning, or whether you could be doing better.

To get the answers I was looking for, I surveyed more than 100 full-time online business owners, and as it turns out, what I discovered was pretty fascinating.

And so, based on that research, here are my biggest insights on what works, what doesn't, and where you should be focusing your time and energy as a blogger or online business owner if you truly want to maximize your efforts and earn a sustainable, long-term income.

EBA Case Study:
Sara Marye, *Stellar Teacher*

EBA student Sara Marye is focused on helping upper elementary teachers. She shares resources, strategies, and offers support and encouragement to make their teaching job easier on her blog, *Stellar Teacher*.

She started selling resources on Teachers Pay Teachers a few years ago, and had experienced some success with that. She realized very shortly after joining TPT that there was great earning potential there, and she decided that if she could make money all while helping teachers that would be a HUGE win! But she wanted to take her business beyond the TPT website to be able to reach teachers in a larger capacity. And that is where EBA comes in, it was not until this past spring that she finally made the leap to launch her own site and dive into EBA.

We love Sara's story because she already had an established business, and therefore a different background and skill set than some of our students who are brand new to the world. BUT what she took away from the course what every bit as powerful. Her biggest "aha moment" was learning how to think like an entrepreneur.

As a teacher, when she started selling her resources on TPT, she was approaching everything she did with a teacher mindset. But EBA really helped her go through a major mindset shift to view herself as an entrepreneur, and to think more like a business woman. From finances, to marketing, to goal-setting, EBA gave her the tools to turn her side hustle into an actual business.

She was able to identify what products were doing well on TPT and create more of what was working, and less of what was not. She was able to identify who she was actually selling to, and have them in mind when creating new products. And because of that, she was able to narrow her focus and rebrand her store which produced an immediate spike in sales!

Sara never imagined that she would leave her teaching job to run her own business, but with the support and tools EBA provided, she was able to focus on the areas that would drive the most results and reach her seemingly impossible goal. And she did it. Within three years of starting her TPT store, she left her teaching job because her income from her own business DOUBLED her teaching salary!

TRAFFIC VERSUS INCOME

Of course, before we can jump straight into what works and what doesn't, we need to have a clear way of defining success. What is the metric that determines whether or not what you're doing is actually working, or whether you are on the right track?

In his incredible book, *Good to Great*, author Jim Collins explains the importance of discovering this defining metric for your business, because it will always tell you whether or not you're actually winning.

When I was first getting started, I just wanted to grow all the numbers. I wanted more revenue, obviously, and I thought that the only way to increase revenue was to increase my traffic. And so I focused heavily on all those metrics that seemed like they mattered—page views, unique visitors, social media followers, etc.

But then I read *Good to Great*, and I realized that I needed a better way of measuring success. And so, as I briefly alluded to in the last chapter, the defining metric that I finally landed on in my business was dollars per visitor.

And let me just tell you—in 2013, when I first started paying attention to this metric, that number was pretty bad—I was earning just $0.03 per visitor. But as I started to focus on it, that number started to go up, first to $0.05 per visitor in 2014, then $0.10 per visitor in 2015, $0.45 per visitor in 2016, all the way up to where it was last year—more than $1.26 per visitor (and still climbing)!

So does more traffic mean more revenue?

The answer is not quite as simple as yes, or no. For the most part, you do need to have at least some traffic or some sort of customer base—preferably an email list—to start earning any real amount of revenue. In my survey, the vast majority of online business owners with fewer than 5,000 monthly page views, or fewer than 5,000 email subscribers earn less than $1000 a month.

But interestingly, as traffic increases, revenue does not necessarily follow. In my survey, I discovered that there are many bloggers and online business owners who are receiving a significant amount of page views—anywhere from 25,000 a month to upwards of 500,000 monthly pageviews—and yet their revenue has remained surprisingly low—less than $5,000 a month in some cases, even as they're receiving more than a *half-million* visitors each month.

That should be a red flag. But surprisingly, for most bloggers, it's not a red flag, or at least it hasn't been until now. I think many bloggers and business owners even think those kind-of numbers are normal, and therefore okay.

And the truth is that those kinds of numbers—high page views with a relatively low income—are in fact "normal." What I found is that most bloggers and online business owners—around 75% of those surveyed—are on a trajectory that earns them, on average, about $0.04 monthly per page view—not much better than what I was earning back in 2013.

But just because this is "normal," doesn't mean this is okay, or that this is what you should be settling for. Because, you see, there are many other bloggers and online business owners on different trajectories, who are earning far more dollars per page views for their efforts.

In fact, from the data I collected, there appears to be five different "zones" when it comes to revenue from your online business.

Zone 1 is the highest zone, and also the rarest, with just 5% of respondents falling in this zone. Business owners in Zone 1 are working incredibly efficiently and earning more than $3.00 per monthly page views to their website.

Zone 2 is the next highest in terms of efficiency and revenue, and also pretty rare, with just 8% of respondents falling in this zone. Business owners in Zone 2 are earning between $1.00 and $3.00 per monthly page views.

Zone 3 comes next, with business owners in this zone earning between $0.50 and $1.00 per monthly page views. And while there are a few more bloggers and online business owners who make it here, Zone 3 still only accounts for about 12% of total respondents.

Zone 4 seems to be the happy medium for many bloggers, with about 35% falling somewhere within this zone. Online business owners within this zone are earning between $0.04 and $0.50 per monthly page view, on average.

Zone 5 is unfortunately where the remaining 40% of bloggers and online business owners seem to be hanging out, earning less than $0.04 per monthly page views. These are the bloggers and online business owners that have fallen into the monetization danger zone that I talked about in the last chapter. They're the ones working hard to grow their traffic—and who might even feel like they're doing okay—but who need to change up their strategy if they really want to maximize their revenue.

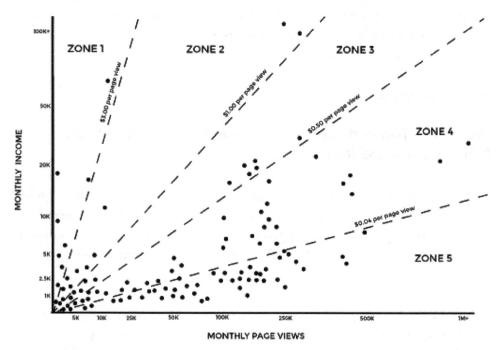

So I guess that begs the question—where does your business fall within these zones? Are you like a full *three-quarters* of bloggers and business owners, hanging out in Zone 4 or 5, working as hard as you can to keep growing your traffic, but not necessarily seeing a good return on all that effort? Or have you figured out how to work smarter rather than harder, and how to focus on the activities that will earn you the most dollars per page view? Have you made it to Zone 1? If not, why not? And what needs to change in your business for you to get there?

THE REVENUE MAXIMIZERS

To answer that question, I think it's helpful to take a closer look at the data, and to specifically look at what those bloggers and online business owners in Zones 1 & 2 are doing differently than those in Zones 4 & 5.

Are there major differences in where revenue is coming from for those two groups? Are there major differences in where they spend their time, or what they focus on? Are there any patterns or trends that seem to be consistent across the bloggers and online business owners who are killing it? Likewise, are there any patterns or trends among the bloggers and online business owners who aren't seeing the best results that you might want to avoid?

Here's what I found:

TREND #1: Top Performers don't worry about ad networks (while bottom performers do).

Of all the patterns and trends that emerged from this study, this was by far the most striking—the fact that the bloggers and online business owners who are generating the most revenue per website visitor generate almost zero revenue from ad networks, while those who are monetizing least efficiently focus almost primarily on ad networks.

As it turns out, fewer than 10% of the bloggers and online business owners in Zones 1 & 2 get any revenue at all from ad networks, and the small percentage that do get any ad network revenue get less than 10% of their total revenue from ads. For the top performers, ads are a non-starter.

Now compare that to the bottom performers in Zones 4 & 5, who tend to focus heavily on ad network revenue. More than half of the bottom performers generate 50% or more of their revenue from ad networks, and nearly a third count ad networks as their only source of revenue.

Bottom Line: Ad networks are not the most effective monetization strategy.

TREND #2: Top Performers focus on products & services.

While the top performers are not concerned with ad network revenue, they are concerned with selling products and services—so much so that for 90% of those in Zones 1 & 2 generate more than 75% of their total revenue from sales of their own products and services.

On the other hand, those in Zones 4 & 5 tend to focus much less on products and services. Two-thirds of bottom performers report that less than 25% of their revenue comes from sales of their own products and services, and nearly half don't sell any products and services of their own.

Bottom Line: Develop your own products and services.

TREND #3: Top Performers are not "Influencers".

Over the past few years, much attention has been given to social media "influencers"—those Instagrammers and YouTubers who work to gain popularity so that they can work with brands or share their favorite products using their affiliate links. And because they're so visible, it is easy to believe that becoming an influencer is vital to online success.

But as it turns out, none of the top performers in our survey would probably be considered an "influencer," at least not on social media. In fact, less than 5% of those in Zones 1 & 2 spend any sort of significant time on social media, with 70% spending less than 10% of their time in that area. Likewise, less than 5% of the top performers generate revenue from working directly with brands.

The bottom performers, on the other hand, are much more focused on keeping up with social media and generating revenue from working with brands. More than one-third of respondents in Zones 4 & 5 report working with brands as one of their revenue streams, and almost half report spending more than 20% of their time on social media.

Bottom Line: You don't need to be "popular" on social media in order to make money online.

TREND #4: Top Performers are not limited to one particular niche, but they're not afraid to narrow in on their target audience.

The top performers were spread across a variety of diverse niches, ranging from education, wellness, and pets to business, crafting, and home décor. On the surface, this didn't seem all that remarkable, given that the variety of niches among the bottom performers were just as diverse.

And yet, amongst the bottom performers, there tended to be a lot more "general" topics. In fact, nearly a third of those in Zones 4 & 5 labeled their niche as "general lifestyle" while another third included other more general topics, such as parenting, food, and personal finance—niches that didn't show up at all among the top performers.

Bottom Line: It's generally more effective to hone-in on a specific niche than to try to be everything to everyone.

TREND #5: Top Performers spend twice as much time on sales & marketing than bottom performers.

On average, the top performers in Zones 1 & 2 spend 20% of their total time focused on sales and marketing, versus an average of only 10% of their total time for the bottom performers in Zones 4 & 5.

On the contrary, the bottom performing bloggers and online business owners in Zones 4 & 5 tend to spend much more time on content creation—an average of 40% of their total time, versus 25% of total time for those in Zones 1 & 2.

Bottom Line: Spend more time selling and less time creating content.

TREND #6: Top Performers are more willing to delegate and hire help, and spend a lot more time on leadership.

Nearly 85% of the top performers in Zones 1 & 2 reported having at least one employee or team member, while less than a third of the bottom performers in Zones 4 & 5 hired any help.

Likewise, the top performers spent an average of 6% of their total time leading and managing the members of their team, while bottom performers spent an average of less than 2% on those types of activities.

Bottom Line: Hiring help can free you up to make more money.

TREND #7: Top Performers don't focus on Amazon.

Finally, it was interesting to note that the top performers in Zones 1 & 2 hardly focused on affiliate revenue at all, and those who did generate any substantial amount of revenue from affiliates tended to work with high-paying programs with generous commission rates, rather than focusing on Amazon.

On the other hand, more than half of the bloggers and online business owners Zones 4 & 5 reported affiliate revenue as one of their main revenue streams, and of those bottom performers who reported affiliate revenue, more than three-quarters included Amazon as one of their top 3 affiliate programs.

Bottom Line: Amazon might be easy, but it's not a great source of revenue.

Keep in mind that while these patterns and trends are helpful to look at, and while they can give us a better idea of where we might want to focus more of our time and attention, it's also important to remember that correlation is not the same as causation. These patterns and trends can help you better understand where you might be going wrong, but they are not the end all, be all in and of themselves.

Overall, though, it's clear that the top performers are doing something differently. They're not chasing page views or worrying about ad network CPMs and Amazon clicks. Instead, they're focused on creating—then selling and marketing—the perfect products for their own unique audience. They don't waste their time trying to be everywhere on social media, but instead focus their energy on growing the metrics that matter.

They're winning. And now you can too.

EBA Case Study:
Monica Froese, *Redefining Mom*

Monica started blogging at *Redefining Mom* in 2013 when her daughter was 9 months old. At the time she knew absolutely nothing about blogging, but knew that she wanted to connect with other moms that were going through similar struggles that she was. She needed a place to feel like that was okay.

As she soon found out, blogging was A LOT of work. But the harder she researched and worked, the more she realized just how much women with blogs were earning. How much SHE could earn.

In March of 2015, the White House reached out to Monica and invited her to participate in a working families event. She was considered to be a member of the press because of her blog. She got invited into the West Wing and met President Obama right outside the Oval office! Her opinions about flexible workplace arrangements and maternity leave were being heard by the most important people in the world—all because she started a blog! Her visit to the White House sparked a renewed interest in using her blog to transform the lives of women around her.

So in 2015, she joined EBA. Her monetization strategy is NOT to chase pageviews. She makes money primarily through affiliate marketing, email marketing, and her own products. However, none of this would have been possible if she did not have a platform to communicate with people—that platform is her blog.

Her strategy is to pull people in from Pinterest (primarily) and get them on her email list. Once they are on her email list, she nurtures them with email sequences, and eventually upsells to an affiliate product, or her own products.

She started EBA in January of 2016, seeing about 7,000 monthly pageviews, 52 email subscribers, and no income. But by February of 2017, just one year after starting EBA and 5 months after quitting her corporate job, she was seeing 64,000 monthly pageviews, had increased her email list to over 10,000, AND acquired her first $10,000 month.

She fully believes that success rests with your email list. Your blog is the start of your funnel and an entry point to bring people to your email list.

So often bloggers get caught up in pageviews and they forget they're missing a key opportunity. But Monica completely honed in on that key opportunity, followed the framework, and is KILLING it!

ADVICE FROM THE TOP PERFORMERS

In addition to collecting data about traffic, revenue, and the way they're spending their time, I also asked the online business owners surveyed to share some of their best advice and insights. They were incredibly candid!

Here's what the top performers had to say:

What is your best advice for someone who is just getting started?

"Dare to dream big. Create a bigger vision for your business than you are comfortable with (dreams are free so what does it matter). But then take time to assign concrete products/steps to achieving that dream... example: you want to make 3-5k a month so you can quit your job. What products/services and how many do you need to sell in order to make that a reality. Having clear steps makes reaching that dream so much easier."

"Make a solid plan first and discuss it with experienced entrepreneurs who have walked the path ahead of you."

"Success in the online world often takes a LOT of time and consistency. You can't put up one or two posts and think you're amazing and you're done. A lot of it is the sucky stuff, and you have to stay with it. Create a team to support you, even if they don't work with you directly, you will need the support! Be kind to everyone, because you don't know how things will play out."

"Build a list and email your subscribers consistently (and prolifically). And remember to keep selling to them too!"

"Every problem has a solution if you look and try hard enough. Be tenacious about identifying and overcoming your challenges every day."

"Get a good strategy on where to spend your time for the most return. You can't do everything, so you might as well do the things that are going to make you the most money."

"Don't be afraid to invest in education for what you don't know, or to invest in hiring help for what you can't do."

"It's important to try lots of things to see what's going to work, but be sure to start and try one thing at a time, and give it time. If it doesn't work, move on to the next idea. Always

have a regular job until you can pay yourself from your side hustle."

"Really, do a business plan—a real one—and market research. Find out what you can actually sell before you get too attached to an idea."

"It's okay to grow slow and take baby steps—they can lead you to incredible places if you take them consistently."

"Work smart. Have a product idea in mind and work towards it with your content instead of just creating content for the sake of creating content."

"Be willing to try many different things. Some will work, some won't. The online world is completely different than the corporate world, you have to make it all up as you go. Be willing to learn from anyone and everyone, even if you consider yourself an "expert."

"All the advice in the world won't take the place of just DOING the things and figuring it out as you go."

"You have to be willing to invest in your business, especially in the beginning. Early on, all of my earnings went back into my business. I invested in courses and tools so that I could grow more quickly."

"Be so very careful who you learn from. Google isn't your best friend when it comes to business."

"I wish I had started building my email list immediately rather than waiting two years to set one up!"

"Build & nurture your email list from day one, make sure everything you do has revenue potential, don't expect it to be easy, and track your time based on ROI."

When you look back on your journey, what was the biggest breakthrough that allowed you to start making real money?

"My breakthrough happened when I had an actual product to sell (and saw that it WORKS)! If a few people are buying this without even knowing me or having a conversation with me, think how many MORE could?"

"Other than EBA, which put me on the right path and gave me an awesome framework, my biggest breakthrough was using my email list to generate revenue. With my email list, I made $1000 in affiliate revenue just a few months after starting EBA, and then when I launched my first product a few months later, I made $15k. Having a strong email list has been the springboard for building revenue."

"It was when I started believing that my services provided value and I increased my prices - you have to believe in yourself or no one else will."

"I worked hard (about 20 hours a week) for 10 months doing basically nothing but trying to build my email list (and sending them weekly emails). I did my first proper product launch of my own digital product, and made $3,000 - enough to cover the $1,000 I had put into the business plus a new iMac. That's when I knew the email marketing really worked."

"Honestly, I think my biggest breakthrough was letting go of my ego. I left my corporate job at the top of my game with 20 years of experience but that doesn't equate to anything in the online world. I had to be willing to accept that few, if any, considered my 20 years as experience—they wanted "real life" and online experience. Although I knew I was capable and it would all translate online, I had to prove myself there and take classes—many of which are not the standard college classes. This means being willing to learn from those younger than you, with different styles than you, and be willing to spend money to build up your knowledge."

"It was when I learned that engaging an audience is 100x more powerful than building traffic."

"My biggest shift happened after I started creating my own products and offering coaching services. I'm not anywhere close to where I want to be on the revenue end yet, but I'm moving in the right direction. Everything is finally starting to come together."

"I think my first breakthrough came when I started hiring out help. I started with a Pinterest VA in the Fall of 2017 and I haven't looked back! Since then, I've hired Graphic Design, Facebook Management, SEO, WordPress Support, and Copy-writing help."

———————

Chapter 8 Action Plan: Do What Works (Skip What Doesn't)

❏ Figure out which monetization zone you are currently operating from, and figure out which zone you most want to be in. What needs to change in order for you to get there?

❏ Based on the research, list your top 3 action items. Where do you most want to be spending your time and energy? What will you focus on?

❏ Choose your favorite piece of advice from the top performers. Place it somewhere where you can see it daily.

chapter 9

You Gotta Make the Ask

"But I don't really want to sell anything. I just want to help people."

I f I had a dollar for every time one of my EBA students said this to me, I'd have a pretty nice pile by now.

Luckily, I make a lot more money from selling things.

And so will you.

But you have to be willing to make the ask.

In the last chapter, I hopefully convinced you why it is so critically important that you create a product—or multiple products—for your audience. Because dollar for dollar, you will be able to earn so much more per reader than by creating your own products than through advertising, or even through most affiliate promotions. If you want to maximize your time and efforts online, there is simply no better way to leverage your platform than by selling your own products.

But even more importantly, when you create your own products, you have the opportunity to create the *exact* solutions that your readers are looking for! And in doing so, you are able to help them more than you would ever be able to while giving things away for free. Because remember—we value what we pay for. If you really, truly want to help people facilitate real change and transformation in their lives, you need to give them an opportunity to invest in themselves.

But just creating that amazing product—one that is perfectly tailored to fit your audience's very specific felt need—is only the *beginning*.

You see, you also have to SELL that product! Because even the best product in the world will just sit there if you don't know how to talk about it, or how to make your readers understand and believe that this product was not only created just for them, it will provide the solution they are looking for.

And that's why, if you are going to be successful, you have to learn how to make the ask. I want you to be completely confident in your sales and marketing skills, and to master the art of getting people to buy whatever it is you are selling.

Because for some unknown reason, a lot of bloggers, authors, and online business owners, look at "sales" and "marketing" as dirty words. They are scared to sell and afraid to market, worrying that they might be perceived as insincere or as a "sellout," or, worse yet, as a little shady or even downright sleazy.

Maybe you're even guilty of some of those thoughts.

Because in addition to the old favorite, "I just want to help people," I can't tell you how many times I've heard my students say, "well I'm just not good at selling," or "selling really isn't my thing," as if somehow that is an excuse or a good reason not to sell.

But here's a little newsflash for you: If you want your business to be successful, you will need to master sales and marketing because *it is your job*. Blogging IS marketing. You can't have a successful, profitable business and NOT sell.

It just doesn't work. And that means you need to make a decision—you are either going to master sales & marketing, you are going to quit, or at least resign yourself to having a non-profitable and time-consuming hobby.

So which is it? Are you blogging just for fun or building a business?

And then repeat after me:

> *Selling is not a dirty word.*
> *Selling is not a dirty word.*
> *Selling is NOT a dirty word!*

You got it? Good.

Okay, so now that I've got the tough love lecture portion of this chapter out of the way, I've actually got some really good news for you. You see, if you've been reading this book in order, and if you've been applying what you've learned, you've already been learning how to master sales and marketing all along the way! You've already laid the groundwork, and you've already begun planting the seeds for your audience. There's actually not that much more that you have to do to pull it all together.

And now that you've laid all the groundwork, you are more than ready to up your sales and marketing game and take it to the next level, which is exactly what we are going to do right now.

I'm going to show you how to pull it all together, by sharing the five essential sales and marketing secrets that every successful blogger or online business owner needs to know. And once you've got these down, you'll truly be unstoppable.

So let's dive in, shall we?

EBA Case Study:
Tasha Agruso, *Kaleidoscope Living*

When Tasha started Elite Blog Academy in 2014, she was a partner in her corporate law firm, where she defended medical professionals in big, multi-million dollar malpractice cases. She was also the mom to three-year old twin girls. To say she was busy and stressed out was an understatement! She started her blog as a hobby to document her home renovations, but then discovered she could earn a living from her business. She ultimately decided to give up her law firm partnership and work on *Kaleidoscope Living* full-time. It's her mission to help people create homes they love, no matter their budgets.

Tasha's primary source of income is selling: both affiliate products and her own (which is not something she necessarily saw herself doing in the beginning). But here is the thing, she followed the steps, saw that she was providing valuable content that her audience was looking for and needed, so they practically told her what to create and she listened!

Any product that Tasha promotes on her platform is one that she has either A) created herself with her readers in mind—like her wildly popular product Designer in a Binder that helps her readers create the home they have always dreamed of without or breaking the bank; or B) products from other companies that she already loves, uses herself, and knows her readers would benefit from.

And she is so successful at it because she has taken the time to build a relationship with her readers; she has listened to their obstacles, earned their trust, and is not just asking them to buy something. She is providing a very real solution. She is offering them a transformation.

GOOD MARKETING STARTS WITH AN AWESOME PRODUCT

When you put in the work of creating a product that is a direct response to the needs of your audience, or when you find a product to promote as an affiliate that you know meets one of the needs of your audience, it's not hard to sell it!

The key is knowing that you've created something, or that you are promoting something that will actually improve their lives or solve their problem.

In your own life, think about the products that you use on a daily basis that you are most passionate and most excited about. Have you ever found yourself telling a friend or a family member about how awesome that product is? Have you ever convinced someone you know to buy something that you have, just because you love it so much?

Sure you have—we all have! My husband, for instance, is completely in love with the squeezable sour cream container that Daisy sour cream came out with a couple of years ago. He's so impressed and excited about it that he will tell anyone who will listen, and now he has all of our friends using it too. He loves the container so much that he doesn't even care that the Daisy brand is almost twice as expensive as the store brand—he just loves that there's no spoon required, no mess, and none of that gross watery stuff at the top.

Is he selling Daisy sour cream? No! He's just talking about something he loves!

I feel the same way about Rent the Runway! I mean how amazing is it to be able to have a constantly rotating selection of amazing designer clothing at your fingertips? I never get bored, and I always look stylish and on-trend—without spending thousands of dollars on clothes! I love it so much that I've actually signed up for two accounts, and I can't tell you how many friends—and blog readers—I've told about how fantastic this service is. I truly love it, and that makes it easy to talk about.

An amazing product—one that solves a problem and fills a need—is easy to get excited about! Your genuine enthusiasm comes through when you talk about it, and it doesn't feel pushy or salesy.

And if you don't feel that way about the product you are trying to promote? Well, then maybe it's not the right product or the right fit for your audience. Always be genuine. If you love something, you'll want to talk about it, and if you don't love it, people will see through you in a heartbeat.

So start with an awesome product—the right product for your audience.

YOU ARE NEVER SELLING A PRODUCT, YOU ARE SELLING A TRANSFORMATION

It's only natural, when you work so hard to create an amazing product, to want to talk about the product, how hard you worked, how much stuff you've included, and how excited (or nervous or scared) you are to get it out there. But honestly, this is where so many bloggers go wrong when they start trying to sell or promote their products, and the reality is that it's all too easy to do!

We get so caught up in the features of the product itself, or talking about our own emotions related to creating the product, that we forget to speak to the felt need.

But no one buys a book because it has 12 chapters, and no one really cares how hard you worked. Instead, people are buying the RESULT they will get from reading that book—the promise of a transformation. They're looking for life to be made easier or improved in some way, to be inspired or uplifted, to be entertained, or to be able to master a skill or gain something that they didn't have before.

When my students decide to enroll in Elite Blog Academy, I can almost guarantee it's not because they're so impressed by the promise of 12 unit videos and 12 unit workbooks and 36 assignments. I'm also quite sure they don't care how many months it took me to write each lesson, or how much work went into producing all those videos, or how exhausted I felt after three straight 12-hour days of filming.

Instead, they enroll in EBA because they're feeling frustrated or overwhelmed with where they're at in their blogging journey. They feel like they're spinning their wheels or having trouble getting traction. They're looking for a step-by-step plan to create a successful, profitable online business, and they are drawn to the promise of having someone who has been there to walk them through every single step.

They may have been swayed by reading or watching success stories from other EBA students who have been through the course and seen the same kind of results they're looking to achieve.

They want the transformation, and that's what they sign up for.

Now does that make me sleazy for highlighting the transformation on my sales page and website, rather than the features and benefits of the course itself? Absolutely not! Remember secret number one? You have to start with an awesome product.

The reason I created Elite Blog Academy in the first place was to solve a real problem—to give overwhelmed bloggers and online business owners a step-by-step framework for creating a successful, profitable, and sustainable online business.

This is exactly what EBA is designed to do, and I know 100% that if you follow the steps I've laid out for you, you will see results. It's not hard for me to promote this course or to talk about the transformation, because I know it works.

And this doesn't just work with courses either. I use the same philosophy whether I am promoting a book, an affiliate product, or even our Living Well Planner®. It's never about the product, it's always about the transformation your customer can achieve after using your product. Focus on that, and selling becomes a whole lot easier!

SELLING IS ALL ABOUT LISTENING, NOT TALKING

Every time I leave to go to a conference or a meeting, my husband again, likes to remind me that I have two ears and one mouth, and that I should use them accordingly.

This is good advice in general, but especially when it comes to selling—you need to listen to what your audience is telling you! When you are busy listening, it is easy to connect the specific needs of your audience to the right solutions. Learn how to mirror the language that your audience is using, and repeat it back to them. Let your customers know you understand and feel their pain, and that you have the solution.

And what's even cooler is that instead of being annoyed by your sales pitch, they will actually thank you for it! I always know we are running a successful sales promotion when I get thank-you emails in return. Because at the end of the day, the most fundamental human need is to feel understood, and to feel like there is someone else out there who gets it, and who gets you.

So take the time to listen to your audience. Pay attention to their struggles, their frustrations, and their concerns. Find solutions and be genuine and generous about sharing them.

EBA Case Study:
Jenny Chauvin, *The Relaxed Homeschool*

Jenny Chauvin runs a blog called *The Relaxed Homeschool* where she helps encourage homeschooling parents. She had a lack of support on her own personal journey, and once she felt secure, she wanted to extend support to others through her website. She started hobby blogging in 2009, but started her homeschooling website in 2014 to work towards helping supplement her family income while helping others.

She began feeling stuck with her newly launched homeschool blog, and decided to jump into EBA in 2014. She knew that she

could do this full-time, she just needed the guidance and support to help her get there. And that is exactly what she found in EBA.

As Jenny continued to grow her blog, she quickly realized that there was an entire community out there (as she expected), that needed exactly what she felt she was missing just years prior. And with that, she started to build a genuine relationship with her audience which proved to be natural, because the obstacles her audience was facing, were still very fresh for her and also things she faced herself.

By being able to really understand her avatar and tap into their feelings, she found herself with the ability to create these products that addressed EXACTLY what her avatar needed. And while the additional income for her family was so appreciated, the reward for Jenny came from the emails that she received in response to her emails. Even the sales emails were thanking her for what she does, and letting her know how her hard work was making a difference in their lives. Not only did she have confirmation that her hard work was paying off, she knew that she had completely nailed her message. She was in tune with her audience and they trusted her—all very important components of growing an online business.

Last year she was close to having her first 6 figure year, and she is confident she will definitely make that goal this year! EBA has shown her the income possibilities, and she's going to keep pushing for higher goals each year.

DON'T BE AFRAID TO ASK

Now while I am all for listening to your audience and for highlighting the transformation, I've also learned that if you want to sell something, there comes a point where you have to actually make the ask.

You can't beat around the bush and be unclear, because truthfully, you aren't doing anyone any favors! If you are starting with an amazing product that you truly believe in, a product you know will help facilitate the transformation that your audience is hoping to get, then be up front and be clear about it!

Flat out say, "you need this product, and here's why."

It's okay to be a little bossy sometimes.

Let's go back to the sour cream example—my husband has no trouble telling our friends they NEED to start buying this sour cream. He doesn't waffle or try to couch his words or sort-of slip it in at the end of a mostly unrelated conversation. He comes right out and tells anyone who will listen, just how great it is. He even takes the container right out of the fridge and does a little demonstration!

Now I know this is probably a silly example—I mean seriously, who is that obsessed about sour cream?—but my point is that no one is annoyed by his directness. They appreciate his enthusiasm, and they all make the switch to Daisy as a result.

But you have to make the ask. You have to be direct.

So don't be afraid to get a little bossy.

PERSISTENCE PAYS OFF

Here's the truth: an effective sales promotion takes TIME. And this is another huge mistake that most bloggers and online business owners make when it comes to promoting a product, whether it's their own or an affiliate's—they mention something once or twice and then wonder why no one's buying.

But the reality is that studies show that on average, it takes eleven exposures to a new product before someone will be ready to buy. ELEVEN. That means you will need to keep talking about whatever it is you are trying to sell for a lot longer than probably feels comfortable.

It also means that you are going to need to plan a full-on blitz attack when it comes to getting the message out there to your audience. One or two emails won't do. You need a whole sequence of emails, paired with blog posts and Facebook ads, and whatever else you can think of.

If you know that the product you are promoting is the right fit for your audience, then don't give up so easily. Keep talking about it. Share your enthusiasm. Be single focused. Speak to your audience's felt need and let them know, under no uncertain terms, that this product is the answer to the problem they are facing, and that it will provide the transformation they are looking for.

———

Chapter 9 Action Plan: Conquer Your Fear of Selling & Start Asking

- ❏ Start with an awesome product. Create something that your audience needs, and that will help them solve an actual problem—hopefully something they're already asking you for.
- ❏ Focus on the transformation—not the features and benefits of your product.
- ❏ Listen to what your customers are telling you, and mirror their language back to them.
- ❏ Don't be afraid to make the ask. It's okay to be bossy.
- ❏ Be persistent. Ask and keep asking, because sales don't usually happen the very first time.

PHASE 4 | BUILD

Up until now, you've mostly focused on the key actions and tactics that are going to help get your online business up and running. This included refining your message by figuring out who you're talking to, what you're going to say, and how you're going to present it. It also meant figuring out how to grow your audience and start building a loyal tribe of people who know, like, and trust you. And then it meant deciding what you'll be selling and how you'll be selling it.

Phase 4, then, is all about bringing all these different elements together, making them better, and building a cohesive, sustainable business. This is where you start working on your mindset and pushing past your limiting beliefs. And it's where you start to see yourself as an entrepreneur, not just a blogger.

In this final section of the book, we'll start by taking a hard look at your mindset and get you mentally prepared to take your business to the next level. We'll then talk about productivity and how to maximize your time most efficiently. Finally, we'll wrap up by talking about how to make that transition from blogger to business owner, what it looks like to make that shift, and what your next steps should be.

chapter 10

Your Mindset Matters

"So, what do you do?"

If someone were to ask you that question right now, what would you say? How do you see yourself, and how do you think of your business? Would you talk about your blog and what it has to offer? Would you identify yourself as a blogger, a mom, a craft enthusiast, or a personal finance expert? Would you still talk about your day job?

However you would introduce yourself, I'm guessing it probably wouldn't be with "I'm a kick-ass entrepreneur growing my own online media empire," or "I'm the CEO and founder of a promising start-up", or even "I run my own online company."

Am I right?

Don't worry, you're not alone. In fact, for years, I dreaded answering that question. I would stumble over my words or try to explain what my blog was about. After I wrote my first book, I found it easier to say I was a writer, and then later a writer and speaker. It took me years before I could say, with confidence, "I own an online media company."

Because blogging is a funny business. So often, it starts as a hobby or a side hustle, something we decide to try just to see how it goes, and just to see if we can. We don't want to take it too seriously, because taking it too seriously and treating it like a real business, well, that would just be scary—not to mention risky. And we might fail. It feels much safer to sit on the side of the pool, dipping our toes into the water. We're not ready to go all in.

But what if I told you that going **all in** *was the only way to make it?*

What if I told you that every single person reading this book *will*, at some point, IF they are to be successful, *fail spectacularly?*

Because the thing is, success only comes through failure and mistakes. Success only comes when you are willing to go all in, and keep going no matter what. Success only comes from blood, sweat, tears, from taking risks—some that will pan out and many that will not—and from working harder than you ever thought was possible. It comes from daring to forge ahead, even when no one is there to guide you, and no one really even understands what it is that you are going for.

And what if I also told you that every single one of you reading this book right now—whether you want to admit it to yourself or not—*is* a kick-ass entrepreneur growing your own online empire?

What would happen if you allowed yourself to believe in that statement?

Because *that* is what I want for you. To take your blog and transform it into a thriving business. To stop seeing yourself as "just a blogger," and instead as a true entrepreneur, and a business-owner—one who takes yourself and your business seriously and who doesn't make excuses for why something can't be done.

To get there, you're going to need to make a few key mindset shifts. You're going to need to embrace a new way of looking at the world, and to start thinking like an entrepreneur.

Because let's face it—entrepreneurs are just a different breed! I know, because I am one. And I am WEIRD. I make my husband crazy sometimes with my big ideas! I scare my team every time I take a few days off, because I always come back with some massive plan that they know is going to be amazing, but also a huge amount of work.

I also know this because I grew up in an entrepreneurial family. My dad was a poor preacher's kid who now owns hotels all over the Pacific Northwest. I even worked in one of those hotels, starting as a bed maker when I was 11 years old. For 8 summers, I worked my way up through the housekeeping ranks until I was finally qualified to work in the laundry room. I can still fold a fitted sheet like nobody's business. It might just be my superpower.

But I digress.

The point I'm making here is that entrepreneurs tend to look at the world in a different way. And if you want to make it as a business owner, you are going to need to start looking at the world in that way too.

THERE ARE NO MISTAKES, ONLY LESSONS

The first mindset shift you're going to have to make is that it is okay to take risks, and even more importantly, that it is okay to make mistakes!! Because there are NO mistakes, only lessons.

Have you ever wondered why we are *so afraid* of making a mistake?

In the course of my research for my book *Do It Scared*®, my team and I surveyed more than 4,000 people about the role of fear in their lives, and specifically about the way fear manifests in their lives, and holds them back from pursuing their biggest goals and dreams.

And as it turns out, not all fears are created equal. My research team and I ended up identifying seven unique Fear Archetypes—seven unique and specific ways that fear affects our lives and personalities. You can take our assessment to discover your own Fear Archetype at assessment.doitscared.com, but in the meantime, do you know what we discovered was the number one most common fear?

You can probably guess.

It's the fear of making a mistake.

It terrifies us, paralyzes us, and prevents us from moving forward. And because we don't want to get it wrong, we procrastinate, obsess over small details, or we stay stuck in the planning stage forever and never actually take the necessary action to make our dreams a reality.

We don't want to fail. We don't want to screw up. We don't want to get it wrong.

But guess what? Screwing up and making mistakes and failing is the most important part of entrepreneurship!! All the learning happens from the mistakes. The biggest breakdowns lead to the biggest breakthroughs.

It's a lesson I've had to learn SO many times. In my early 20's, during my senior year of college, I had a complete mental breakdown. I attempted suicide multiple times, was diagnosed with major depression and PTSD, and spent more than two years in and out of psychiatric hospitals. My life literally fell apart, and I ended up divorced, bankrupt, and all alone. At 23, I felt like I had screwed up my life forever.

But then my dad gave me a chance. That one little chance he gave me, despite the fact that everyone else had given up, was a job working the weekend breakfast shift at one of his hotels, and I started to get a little confidence back. That job led to a better job, and then an even better one, and eventually I worked up enough confidence to go back to school, finish my degree, and apply to law school.

But then I dropped out of law school and had to learn that lesson all over again. I had worked SO hard to put my life back together, and I was terrified that dropping out would mean I was a failure, that I couldn't hack it, and that I was never going to be successful. I felt like I was giving up on my dream, and giving up on myself.

And it hurt. A lot. I wasn't sure I would ever find my way again.

But then another opportunity came along, this time the opportunity to manage a large day spa, one that was losing a lot of money—more than $50,000 a month—and needed a lot of help turning things around. I was so hungry to prove myself! I thought it would be my big chance. My chance to finally make something of myself, and finally be successful in life after having screwed up so many times.

But you know what? I failed again.

I couldn't save the spa. Either I wasn't good enough, or maybe it just wasn't possible. Either way, it was pretty devastating. A mistake that almost broke me, in more ways than one.

But ultimately, it *didn't* break me.

Life went on, and as time went on, I started to look back on the lessons I learned during that disaster of an experience, with gratitude instead of bitterness.

And by the time I started a business of my own, I knew that I had nothing to fear, because failure just didn't seem that scary anymore. I had been there and done that. And more importantly, from all those failures, I had learned a whole lot of things NOT to do.

Of course that's not to say I don't still make mistakes—I do! All the time. In fact, practically on a daily basis. Some of them are big, painful mistakes that end up costing us a lot of money and heartache. Others are smaller mistakes that are upsetting in the moment, but usually good for a laugh later on.

Seriously, once we accidentally sent out an email to our entire email list that had the URL *www.xxx.com* in it—those x's were meant to be a placeholder, but someone forgot to insert the real URL, and then no one tested the link, and before you know it, we had sent 400,000 people the link to a porn site (don't go to that URL, I'm warning you!). Yep, we sure did.

I really, *really* wish I was joking.

I also wish I could say that was the last time we ever made an email mistake. But at the end of the day, email is not life or death. No one is going to die if an email is late or if a link is messed up. And sometimes you just have to be okay with a few mistakes. Because mistakes are where all the learning happens.

And not allowing yourself to make mistakes—that is actually the biggest mistake you could ever make as a business owner. Because it means you're not taking risks. You're not daring to try new things. You're not putting yourself out there. You're not going all in. And without the risk, there will be no reward.

IT'S NOT PERSONAL, IT'S BUSINESS

The second mindset shift you'll need to make is knowing that it's not personal—it's business.

And this is sometimes a really hard one to accept, especially for women. Because often in the types of businesses we tend to start, especially with blogging and writing, podcasting or videos, or even things like consulting and direct sales, it does feel personal. You're sharing snippets and stories from your own life. You're making yourself vulnerable and putting yourself out there. You are visiting people in their homes, or posting on social media. You are opening yourself up to criticism and complaints and snarky comments and unfiltered feedback.

And that all feels pretty personal sometimes.

But here's the thing—if you're going to go all in with this business thing, you'll need to figure out how to put on your big girl panties (or your big boy briefs) and stop worrying about how you're being perceived and just get out there and do the work that needs to be done. If putting yourself out there is part of that job, then so be it. And if you approach it from a "this might be uncomfortable for me personally, but this is going to make my business stronger, more successful, or better in some way", then *do that thing*.

Let your drive to make your business AWESOME be the thing that overrides your fear of putting yourself out there, and the thing that allows you to separate your feelings from your business.

Because here's the hard truth—as a business owner and an entrepreneur, and as the CEO of your company, you don't get the luxury of having feelings or getting emotional, or even having a bad day. Sometimes you just have to suck it up, buttercup, and keep that smile on your face no matter what.

And I'm not going to lie. That's hard sometimes. Brutal even! It really sucks when you have an employee take advantage of you, or when you find out a bunch of people you thought were your friends are badmouthing you behind your back. It sucks when your product launch flops, when you make a bad hire, or when your expenses are way higher than your income in a given month. Being a business owner doesn't make you immune to feeling sad, scared, or lonely sometimes. I promise that it only gets harder scarier and lonelier, the bigger and more successful your business becomes.

But those are just the breaks.

There's no crying in baseball, and there's no crying in business either.

Because let me tell you something—the bloggers that are whining on Facebook that someone was mean, that someone else stole their idea, that a reader or customer sent them a nasty email, or that one of their employees did something to tick them off—those people will only ever JUST be bloggers or influencers or side hustlers. They're

189

making it personal. And it's not personal. It's business.

And speaking of side hustles, commit to treating your business like a real business, even from the very beginning—even when it is still just a side hustle.

Because if you tell yourself that it's NOT a real business, that it's just a personal thing, something you are doing for fun or to pass the time, you never have to take it too seriously. You never have to commit to the drive, and the blood, and the sweat and the tears. You'll end up spending your time complaining about all the haters and badmouthing the people who are actually making it happen.

Or you can get to work and, as my friend Tasha Agruso likes to say, "start drinking those tears of your haters."

It's your choice.

NO ONE ELSE KNOWS WHAT THEY'RE DOING EITHER

Your third mindset shift is to understand, once and for all, that no one else really knows what they're doing either.

And trust me—this is so true!

All those people you are looking up to? All those people who seem like they've got it all figured out, who are totally rocking and rolling, who seem to always know exactly what their next step should be, always seem to take exactly the RIGHT steps in the RIGHT direction, and who always seem to be in the RIGHT place at the RIGHT time, who know all the RIGHT people......

NONE of them knows what they are doing either!

We're all just *making it up* as we go along!

Because in the end, *that's what entrepreneurship is.*

It took me quite a while to realize this. For so long, I was so convinced that everyone else had it figured out, and I was just pretending to know what I was doing. I spent hours reading every word every single person of "authority" had to say, never once stopping to question whether or not the person, or people, I was listening to actually had any clue what they were talking about.

But then, in my early years of blogging I got invited to join what, at the time, seemed like a very prestigious collaboration of personal finance bloggers, sponsored by a fairly big company.

Being the baby blogger that I was, I thought I had *made* it. I couldn't believe they asked me to join this group, and I really couldn't believe it when they flew me and the 30 or so other bloggers in this group to New York City for an all-expenses paid retreat. It felt like a dream.

And then, a few months later, I was practically pinching myself when this same company decided to roll out a whole new initiative, and they called to personally invite me to be part of the initial rollout for this program. I had made it into the *super* elite group within this elite group, and I was sure that this was my big break.

But there was a hitch.

You see, there was a small clique of four women in this group who wielded a LOT of power. They ran the Facebook group that "everyone" hung out in, and they had even started their own blogging conference. Their blogs were well-established and well-known, and if it had been junior high (and believe me, sometimes it felt like it), those women would have been the popular girls, the girls that every other girl wanted to be.

Unfortunately, from the moment we met, during what turned out to be a *painfully* awkward sushi dinner in New York City, these four women just did *not* like me. I don't know why. This wasn't in my head—one of them actually told me so. Maybe they thought I didn't deserve to be there. My brand-new blog was nothing compared to theirs. Maybe they thought I was too tall. Maybe they were just mean girls. All these years later, I still have no idea.

But they were pretty powerful, or at least it seemed that way at the time, and this group of four convinced the company I had been invited to work with, to hire them to run this new initiative.

Once in charge, the first thing they did was un-invite me.

I was out in the cold. And I was *devastated*.

I felt like my life was over. I had been sure that this was my hot ticket to success, and just like that, it was gone, without any recourse.

I cried for days, until finally my husband just couldn't take it anymore.

"Why do you even care what those mean girls think of you," he said. "*Who cares* what everyone else is doing? This is not the end all to your business. In fact, you're *way* better off doing your own thing. So suck it up and just go be *you*."

And he was right.

Thankfully, I decided to take his advice. I withdrew from the group and stopped trying to emulate what everyone else in my field was doing, and I started totally doing my own thing.

As a result, my business grew exponentially.

What's more, every person I spoke to who actually participated in that initiative, the one from which I was disinvited, absolutely *hated* it. In fact, for many of them, it ended up being a year-long distraction that didn't grow their businesses as promised, and made them very little money. While my business was taking off, they were standing still. A few of them even quit altogether.

That could have been me.

Instead, it was the moment I realized that not only is it okay to do your own thing, but that most of the time, it is much, *much* better.

The longer I am in business, the more I realize how much it is true. And over the years, I have gotten a lot better at trusting my gut and continuing to just throw spaghetti against the wall until something sticks.

Even so, I'm still not immune to looking at the people who are further ahead than me, and thinking that they've somehow got it all figured out. I'm not immune to falling for the next big trend that "everyone" is all excited about, only to have it be nothing but a giant distraction from my goals, and a huge waste of time.

But do you know what I discover every time I actually sit down to talk to one of those people who from afar seem like they have it all figured out? I discover that *they don't know what they're doing either!* Oh sure, we can all look back on what we've done and figure out what worked… in the past.

But the future? The next step? It's always a mystery. It's always a guess. It's always taking a risk and stepping into the unknown. It's always trying something new, and then something else, and then something else after that. It's testing and trying and putting yourself out there. Again and again and again.

Because that is what being an entrepreneur is all about.

LOOK FOR A ROLE MODEL, NOT A RESCUER

It's only natural, when faced with the unknown, or when trying to do something you've never done before, or when feeling unsure, to look for a role model or someone else to guide you along the way. Because let's face it, in any endeavor in life, it is nice to have someone who has been there, who just gets it, and who knows exactly what you are going through. It's helpful to have someone offering up their wisdom and advice, and possibly even showing you exactly what to do.

And that's true no matter what you might be going through. There's nothing more reassuring for a new mom, than another mom offering first hand advice on everything from feeding to teething, and sleeping through the night. Likewise, there's nothing more helpful to an entrepreneur than talking or listening to other more experienced business owners.

No one wants to feel like they are going it alone, wading into uncharted territory all by themselves. It's comforting to be able to follow in someone else's footsteps, and reassuring to know that whatever you are trying to do *is* actually possible, because someone else has done it.

In general, role models and teachers and mentors and coaches are a good thing— especially when it comes to doing it scared.

And so, if you are preparing to break out of your comfort zone and try something new, then finding someone to guide you along the way can be a really smart idea. That person can help you avoid pitfalls and let you know that you are on the right track. It might mean taking a class, hiring a coach, or just talking to someone who has already done the thing that you want to do.

But there's a catch.

You see, a role model is someone that *you* seek out for guidance, not the other way around. And that is a very different scenario than simply hoping for someone else to figure it out for you, or to show you the way. Looking for a role model is not the same thing as waiting to be rescued.

And it is really, really important to understand the difference.

When you actively seek out a role model for guidance, you are assuming responsibility and taking ownership of your journey. You are being proactive, not reactive, and you understand that the job of your role model is not to do the work for you, but to show you that it can be done and to offer guidance along the way.

On the other hand, when all you do is wait for a rescuer, or sit around wishing and hoping that someone would help make things easier, you are allowing yourself to be the victim. What's worse, you are giving away all your power to someone who may or may not ever show up.

I guarantee that you do not need to be rescued, but you might need a role model. Luckily for you, there are role models, teachers, coaches, and mentors everywhere you look—you just have to start looking.

BE WILLING TO JUST START

The final mindset shift you'll need to make is to always be willing to just start, even when you don't have all the answers.

You can't wait for the moment to be right, because it never will be. Don't wait until you feel like you know exactly what you are doing, because you never really will.

Just start. Right here, right now, totally imperfectly, without knowing exactly how it is all going to end. You don't have to know all the steps before you begin, and you don't have to know exactly how it is all going to play out.

You just have to take the next step. Or the first one.

You've got to do it scared.

Because here's the thing—action is the antidote to fear.

Every time you step outside your comfort zone, every time you take just one tiny step in the right direction, you build up a little more courage and more confidence for the next move.

So take action. Just start. Because any action is better than none!

———————

Chapter 10 Action Plan: Fix Your Mindset

❏ Begin thinking of yourself as an entrepreneur (and a kick-ass one at that), rather than just a blogger.

❏ Be willing to take risks, and adopt the mantra that there are no mistakes, only lessons.

❏ Don't make it personal, because it's not personal, it's business.

❏ Realize that we're all just making it up as we go along.

❏ Look for a role model, not a rescuer.

❏ Take action, even when you're not totally confident in the steps you need to take. Action is the antidote to fear!

Chapter 11

Work Smarter, Not Harder

"Don't you know we all get the same 24 hours?"

It was a life lesson I've never forgotten, wisely shared by my friend Melissa, who had just spent at least fifteen minutes listening to me go on and on about another friend of ours, who somehow seemed to have her whole life in order—while I felt like I was struggling to do anything right.

Melissa gently reminded me that no one can do it all, and that just because someone's life looks perfect from the outside looking in, doesn't mean that's always the case.

"You have to choose," she said, *"what's going to be most important to YOU. You have to decide which balls you're going to keep in the air, and which ones you're going to drop. You've got to know your priorities. We all get the same amount of time, but how you decide to spend it is up to you."*

There are only 24 hours in a day. And at this point, you might be feeling totally overwhelmed at the thought of trying to make it all work. You might be wondering how you, one person with kids, or a job, or a whole list of pre-existing obligations could possibly find the time to keep up with everything you've already got going on, and still get an online business off the ground.

The simple answer is this: You can't.

If you try to do everything all at once you will either make yourself crazy, drive those around you crazy, or completely burn out before you even start. You might even manage to do all three. In any case, it won't get you very far.

You have to choose. You have to decide what's going to be most important to you right now.

When it really comes down to it, starting an online business is a marathon, not a sprint. You have to be in it for the long haul and to keep telling yourself that the work put in on the front end will pay off eventually. If you try to rush it, you may be setting yourself up to crash and burn. If you don't make it a priority, you'll risk languishing in a sea of uncertainty forever. And you also have to be strong enough to not listen to the people who don't get it, who tell you that you're wasting your time.

That said, there are lots of ways to work smarter in order to maximize your efficiency and get more done in less time. You may still not be able to do it all, but you will be able to do a lot more than you think.

BECOME A BETTER GOAL SETTER

I've always loved setting goals, but I haven't always been the best at following through on those goals. What used to happen is that I'd start out strong, for the first couple of weeks, with lots of enthusiasm. But then I'd start to lose focus and start to slip, or something would go wrong, or it would get hard, and all my amazing intentions went straight out the window. The excitement was over.

And so, for many years, most of my goals and resolutions were just like everyone else's. Platitudes that made me feel good for a few days or weeks, but nothing that I could actually look back on a year later and feel like I totally rocked it.

That was frustrating because I WANTED to be rocking those goals. And I wanted to be accomplishing big things in my life. But I could tell that I just wasn't getting clear enough on what I needed to accomplish, and I wasn't doing a good job of staying focused and keeping my big goals top of mind.

Then, in April 2013, I decided to completely change my strategy towards setting goals. You see, I had actually set some goals for myself at the beginning of the year, but by the time April rolled around, most of them, once again, had fallen by the wayside. But that month was a big month for our family, because it was the month when my husband Chuck quit his job to become our household's stay-at-home parent, so that I could focus on growing my business full time.

And let me just tell you—suddenly having the pressure of being the primary breadwinner for our family, and not JUST being the breadwinner, but supporting our family through a BLOG, this thing that I had started from scratch, and this business that I was just making up as I went along—well, that pressure lit a fire under my butt like never before. It was a pressure like I have never felt before.

Because up until that moment, everything I was doing was just for fun. If I failed, well, so what? My husband had a great job and we would be fine.

But now it was all on me. All of it. Not just going to work and collecting a paycheck, but actually figuring out how to make this blogging thing a sustainable business that could continue to support us for the long term.

I'm going to be completely honest with you—I was *terrified*. At that point I had no real reason to believe that anything that I was doing, that any of the money I was making, was anything other than a fluke. I was so worried that it could all go away at any minute, and I wanted to make as much money as I could as fast as I could so that we didn't go broke in the process.

But it was in that pressure cooker that I realized I needed to do something different with my goals. I needed to figure out a way to get super focused, and to STAY focused, so that I could actually accomplish big things and make more sustainable progress. I needed to start looking at the big picture a little bit more, and start doing those big things that were going to move the needle and help support my family; rather than just trying to keep up on all the day to day busywork.

So you know what I did?

I created a planner for myself. It was pretty basic and pretty ugly, but it was a planner that first of all had a page for my long term goals, and then monthly sections that included monthly goals, as well as a month at a glance page, and weekly planning pages, and some other pages that more related to blogging stuff. And then I had the whole thing printed out at Staples, and I had the back and front covers laminated, and then had it coil bound.

And I am not exaggerating when I tell you that this one simple thing was probably the biggest game changer in my entire business, and maybe even in my entire life. In fact, within two months of starting to use this planner, I literally tripled my revenue, and six months later, I had not only accomplished ALL of the big goals that I set out to do, but for the first time ever, I felt like I was working towards something that was sustainable, and that could actually last.

So what was it exactly that made all the difference? Well, to be honest, it was making a few incredibly simple but key changes, not to the goals that I set, but how I defined and measured success, and how I tracked my progress.

Narrow Your Focus

The first really big change that I made was to stop trying to do everything, and to narrow my focus to just the most important things. You see, I was one of those people who tended to set really vague, generic-sounding goals that basically covered everything under the sun. And what's more, I would set a WHOLE BUNCH of really vague, generic-sounding goals.

It was just a bunch of fancy-sounding platitudes, but there was nothing specific to grab onto, and there was certainly no focus.

My list might as well have said blah. Blah blah blah blah blah blah blah blah.

But when forced to buckle down and really focus, I realized that I needed to hone-in and get a lot more specific about what I wanted to accomplish. Not only that, I needed to limit myself to just a handful of very specific goals, instead of having a whole list of generic platitudes that actually meant nothing.

And so, that's what I did. I sat down and identified the five major goals I needed to accomplish by the end of the year in order to take my business to the next level. For me, in 2013, that list included these 5 things:

1. Secure a book deal with a traditional publisher
2. Write and self-publish a book of my own
3. Write a 31-day series on my blog
4. Speak at a conference
5. Begin working with brands in a meaningful way

And guess what? I found that once I narrowed my focus, I suddenly became a lot more clear about some of the big things that I needed to do. Instead of spending every day in the weeds, I was setting time aside for bigger projects—things like writing a book proposal, networking with brands, and writing and self-publishing my own book. Before this, those things were all just ideas floating around in the back of my mind, not things I was actually serious about.

What I've learned in the years since then, is that when it comes to your big goals for the year, narrowing your focus and honing in on your MOST important goals is super key. That first year I picked five things, but these days I force myself to pick just 3 major goals for the year—the goals I call my "big 3."

And the reason for that is simple—when you only have 3 goals, it's a lot easier to remember them.

Last year, for instance, my 3 big goals were to launch a podcast, to write a new book, and to lose 25 pounds. And you know what? If I had accomplished nothing else the entire year, the fact that I did just those 3 things was more than enough!

So that's the first change to make if you want to start setting goals that you will actually accomplish—narrow your focus. Don't set a whole bunch of ambiguous goals; instead, pick just a few specific things that you really want to do.

Pick Goals that You Actually Care About

The biggest thing I've learned about goals and about staying motivated enough to actually follow through on your goals is that your WHY needs to be bigger than your fear, and bigger than your resistance to it. You need to WANT IT more than you are scared of it, and more than you don't feel like doing a certain thing.

That was definitely true for me in 2013, after my husband had left his job and I became the sole breadwinner in our family. Suddenly my motivation to do really hard things—things I probably would have resisted earlier—was super high. My WHY was not wanting to see my family end up out on the street because I couldn't hack it as a business owner.

What I have learned in the years since, is that the more connected I am to the WHY behind a goal, the more likely I am to follow through. When I try to set goals that I think I'm supposed to do, or goals that other people encouraged me to do, I'm not really that motivated. Now maybe that's just my Outcast nature, but no matter what your Fear Archetype, it's important to understand what motivates you and what is important to you, and to connect that goal to what is most important to you.

If you are more of a People Pleaser, you might realize the thing that motivates you most is the fear of letting other people down. And if that's true, then you need to figure out a way to connect your goal to other people's expectations. If you are a Procrastinator, you might need to be motivated by a hard deadline that forces you to take action. If you're a Rule Follower, you might need a step by step plan that has been outlined by someone in authority, like a coach or a mentor. (Again, you can find out your own Fear Archetype at assessment. doitscared.com.)

But pick goals that mean something to you, and that you actually care about. They are YOUR goals—they have to be something you actually want to accomplish, or else what's the point?

Define What Success Looks Like For You

For this, I use a process called Goal Crushing®, because it really helps me to first, get clear about what it is that I am really aiming for, and what I want to accomplish, then it gets me clear on what steps I have to take to get there, what potential obstacles I need to be prepared for, what success actually looks like, and how I'll celebrate.

The process is pretty simple, and corresponds with the acronym CRUSH IT.

That's C-R-U-S-H-I-T.

C stands for claim your target—that just means knowing what it is that you want to accomplish.

R stands for refine your objective. And this means to get clear and specific about your measures of success—dates, metrics, etc. It's turning your vague goal into something that you can objectively measure.

U stands for understand your motivation. And this is something we've already talked about, but is good to reiterate—understanding your why, and what about this goal really matters to you.

S stands for step it out. And this is where you identify all the things that need to happen in order for this goal to be successful. From there,

H stands for handle obstacles. This means identifying the potential roadblocks that might trip you up, and creating a plan to deal with them before they actually happen.

I stands for implement your plan. This means taking action, but also understanding the danger that you face if you don't follow through. Finally,

T stands for treat yourself. And this is where you identify how you'll celebrate your win, which will help keep you motivated for the next goal!

This Goal Crushing worksheet is actually found in each monthly section of our Living Well Planner®, which is the planner that eventually evolved out of that first blog planner I created for myself back in 2013. However, if you don't use the planner, or you just want more of them, we also have a PDF version that you can get in our shop at livingwell.shop.

And the thing is, it might seem weird that a one page worksheet can do so much, but it really can. It's sort of amazing that way. It's just this really easy way of getting complete clarity about what you are aiming for and what you need to do to get there.

So get specific and define what success looks like for you—that's the third change you'll need to make to be a truly effective goal setter.

Keep Your Goals Top of Mind

This means figuring out what it's going to take, to keep your goals right in front of you throughout the year, so you don't forget about them.

There are LOTS of ways you can do this. For me, I love having them in the front of my planner. That way they're always right there in front of me, and then each time I plan my goals for the month, I am careful to make sure that I am working on at least a piece of that big goal for the year. Other ways I like to keep my goals top of mind for the year is to create a desktop background that has them on there, and to also make it the screen saver for my phone.

I know people who write them on their bathroom mirror, who have a big board above their desk, or who put a chalkboard up in the living room that lets them see their big goals every single day. Maybe it will be sharing your goals with an accountability partner or life coach and meeting regularly with that person to report your progress.

Whatever it is that is going to remind you, each and every day, of what you are aiming for—do that. Do everything you can to keep that goal fresh in your mind, the reminder of what you are aiming for.

Because make no mistake—you WILL need the reminder. Again and again and again. As humans we are constantly distracted, which is why it is so important to not only get clear about where you want to go, but to put safeguards in place and keep your goal at the front of your mind.

STAY ORGANIZED

Between post ideas, income from thirty-seven different sources, important contacts, traffic statistics, social media, photos, craft supplies, recipes, schedules, deadlines, expenses, and everything else blogging related, staying organized can easily become totally overwhelming. There is just so much to keep track of!

I'll be the first to admit that I'm kind-of a planning junkie. In fact, over the years I've tried many different planners, calendars, Google docs, and spreadsheets to stay organized.

But truthfully, I can't even imagine growing the business that I have WITHOUT being completely vigilant about setting goals, planning ahead, being diligent about setting my priorities, and managing my time well.

Creating my first blog planner—strictly for my own use—in 2013 was a complete game changer for my business. That's when I first got serious about setting goals, measuring progress, and planning my time, and that's exactly when my business started to take off.

But in 2015, I started looking for a better solution.

You see, I truly believe the biggest reason my blog planner was SO effective in helping grow a successful business was that it helped me to set long term goals, and then to break down those long-term goals into monthly goals.

Yes, it had some features unique only to blogging, such as a brainstorming page and a stat tracking page, but at some point, I realized that most of the stats I was tracking were vanity metrics anyway, and that I preferred brainstorming on Post-it notes.

But I also realized that when it came to managing my whole life, the blog planner didn't quite cut it. So much was slipping through the cracks—things like staying on top of my entire schedule, not just my blog schedule, keeping track of my budget, planning my meals, and setting goals that weren't just blog-related.

Something had to give.

And so, I decided to create a new planner—one that would help me organize my *whole life*, not just my blog. After all—I'm more than just a blogger. I'm also a wife, a mom, a friend, and a *person*.

And ultimately, that is how the Living Well Planner® was born.

So much more than just a blog planner, it was the sanity-saver I needed to take my business—and my life—to the next level. And while you might not be a paper planner kind-of person (and that's okay), I do recommend using some of the features found in the Living Well Planner to help keep yourself organized and manage your time more effectively.

Long-Term Goals

Setting long-term goals helps take you out of the day-to-day busywork of just trying to stay on top of the next blog post or social media engagement and focus on the bigger picture. What do you hope to accomplish as a blogger? What is your endgame? Where do you see yourself in one, five, or even ten years? It is pretty amazing how much more you can accomplish when you approach your daily task list with the perspective of how it will help you reach your long-term goals. It makes prioritizing and separating the essential from the time fillers much, much easier.

Setting a small number of very clear goals is really the ultimate game changer. It gives a focus and a direction that you wouldn't otherwise have, and it keeps you from chasing too many squirrels. They become your compass.

Year at a Glance

After you've set your big goals for the year, it's a good idea to dive into the nitty gritty and spend some time actually planning out what that will look like from a practical standpoint, week-to-week. The Year at a Glance spread is perfect for that, because you can break down the whole year week-by-week, and know exactly what will be going on at any given time. This keeps you from getting "stacked" with too many projects happening at once.

Monthly Goals

Monthly goals are the medium-term goals that help break down long-term goals into manageable chunks and help you focus your priorities. Because while big goals are great, this monthly goals page is where the real magic happen because it forces you to revisit those big goals every single month, and to break them down into smaller pieces that will get you closer to the finish line. It's pretty amazing to look back and see how you were able to accomplish seemingly insurmountable tasks, just by taking them a little bit at a time.

Goal Crushing

I recommend breaking down at least your single biggest goal for the month using our Goal Crushing® formula. I promise you will be amazed at how much more clarity and focus you have after taking the time to do this!

Month-at-a-Glance (Editorial Planning)

The monthly calendar is the perfect place for keeping track of major events, as well as for planning your editorial calendar.

Weekly Planning

Planning out your week is where it all gets real, and to be honest I don't think that there has been any habit more transformative in my own business, or my life, than taking the time to block out my time each week, along with 10 minutes each day to set my intentions.

I usually plan for the following week on Friday afternoons, so that I can go into the weekend knowing that I've got a plan to take care of all those tornadoes that would normally be spinning around in my brain.

I start my planning session by doing a quick brain dump of everything that I know I'll need to work on the following week. Then I prioritize those tasks into A, B, & C tasks using my Weekly Wizard™ sticky notes (available at livingwell.shop).

From there, I block out time in my schedule to accomplish everything I need to do. I start by making time for the A tasks—the biggest, most important things that will get me closer to my goals. Next, I make time for my B tasks—those things that are important but not "big goal" important. Finally, if there is any space left, I make time for my C tasks—the things I'd like to do if I can fit them in.

And then every morning I fill out my Daily Do-It™ sheet with my prioritized task list for the day, so I know exactly what to focus on. And while all this might seem like a lot of time for planning, I would estimate that it actually saves me at least 20 hours a week. I'm never spinning because I know exactly what needs to happen next.

DO THE MOST IMPORTANT THINGS FIRST

I read a book a few years ago that totally changed the way I approached my daily task list. It was called *Eat That Frog: 21 Great Ways to Stop Procrastinating and Get Things Done* by Brian Tracy. It got its name from a quote by Mark Twain, who famously once said something to the effect of, "if you eat a frog for breakfast, chances are that will be the worst thing you have to do all day." The point of the quote—and the book—was that if you start your day by tackling your hardest but most important tasks, even if you don't do that much for the rest of the day, you will still have accomplished a lot.

In blogging, it is really, really easy to get sucked into the time-wasting vortex of social media and email. They seem so important, so urgent, but before we know it, we've spent the whole day reacting to other people rather than proactively reaching our own goals. In my own experience, I found that when I stopped checking email first thing in the morning, and instead focused those first few hours of my day on writing and long-term projects, my productivity skyrocketed and I was finally able to start meeting my bigger goals.

Here are a few more time-management strategies that have helped me the most:

Stick to a daily routine. The more good habits you can create when it comes to blogging and working efficiently, the easier it will be to get things done. Our brains are pretty amazing, and although it initially takes a lot of willpower to create a new habit or routine, after a few weeks that behavior starts to go on autopilot. Starting your day in the same way each morning will tell your brain that it is time to work.

Make a daily checklist. My own morning routine always starts with devotions, then a cup of coffee as I plan my task list for the day. I try to list my tasks in the order that I want to accomplish them, starting with the hardest and most essential tasks to my long-term goals. I use my Daily Do It to make my list for a couple of reasons. First, it is small enough to keep my list manageable, and second, it sticks nicely to my current weekly planning page in my Living Well Planner.

Set the timer. Giving yourself a certain amount of time to work on each task helps keep you motivated and on task. I usually just put a time in parentheses after each task on my list.

Take regular breaks. Our brains can work at any given task for about 90 minutes before we start to fade and get distracted. Taking a quick 5–15 minute break to get up and stretch, drink a glass of water, or have a snack before getting back to the grind can make a huge difference.

Delete the unessential. If the number of things on your to-do list is far more than you can realistically get done, or the number of emails coming in is far more than you could ever possibly respond to, it is time to start deleting. While it is tempting to try to tackle the "easy" tasks or emails first, a smarter approach is to remove anything on your list or in your inbox that doesn't line up with your overall long-term goals. Time is precious; don't waste it on the stuff that doesn't matter.

Work in bulk. I've alluded to this one already in earlier chapters, but if you tend to do a lot of the same type of posts, such as DIY projects or recipes, it is far more efficient to plan, create, and photograph multiple posts at the same time. That way you can shop once, cook or create (and make a big mess) once, then upload and sort photos once. I will generally try to do at least a month's worth of DIY projects or recipes in one day, which ends up saving me a lot of time later on.

Use canned responses. If you get a lot of the same type of questions or emails, taking the time up front to set up canned responses in Gmail can save you a *lot* of time and energy when it comes to tackling your inbox each day. **Turn off all alerts.** It is a lot easier to resist the ding of email alerts, Facebook, Instagram, or Skype messages if you simply can't hear them. This goes for push notifications on your phone as well!

Save the mindless stuff for later in the day. Willpower and discipline are finite resources, which means we tend to have less to draw on as the day goes on. Save your easy, more mindless tasks—such as responding to email, interacting on social media, and catching up on blog reading—for the time of day when you feel the least motivated.

Chapter 11 Action Plan: Work Smarter, Not Harder

- ❏ Develop a system of staying organized—whether it be with a blog planner, series of folders, a virtual calendar, or something else.
- ❏ Set concrete, quantifiable, long-term goals. Write them down!
- ❏ Improve your time management skills and do the important things first.

Chapter 12

From Blog to Business

"I think I finally get it. My blog is not my business. It's just a tool I can use to grow my business. Now I realize I'm looking at it all wrong!"

After four days of intense workshopping at my company headquarters in Florida, Tamara finally had an epiphany. It was the moment she realized that the blog she had been working so hard on—the blog she had thought was her business—was really just the marketing tool she was using to *grow* her business.

In an instant, she realized that she had been missing the point—focused on trying to write a little bit about everything in order to get more views on her page, when she needed to be focused on creating products, then using her blog as a way of attracting the customers who most needed that particular product.

It was a revelation, and one that changed everything.

At some point, if you've followed the advice in this book, your blog will start earning some money. Perhaps it already has. It might start slowly at first, with just a small trickle of affiliate commissions or your very first painfully small AdSense check. You'll write an e-book that starts to build steam, or get approached by a brand to do your first paid endorsement. And before you know it, this thing that you built from nothing with your own two hands, this *blog*, will actually be generating a real income.

When that finally happens, it is a very sweet moment indeed.

But if you can't make the shift from blogger to business owner, you'll always be selling yourself short.

Because the truth is that if your blog has developed to the point that it is generating an income, you are no longer just a blogger, you are an *entrepreneur*. And your blog is not a business; it is one of the *assets* of your business. It may be the biggest asset and the most significant asset, but it is only *one* of the assets. And I would dare to guess that your business probably has many other assets you may not have necessarily considered.

In this book, we've covered a lot of ground together so far, from refining your message to growing your audience, to monetizing your platform and now to building your business. You've laid a solid foundation for building your successful, profitable blogging business; one that is set up for long-term growth and sustainability.

And now, in this final chapter, before I send you out into the world of online business all on your own, I want to spend some time talking about leadership, and about what it means to be an effective CEO of your company.

Because, like it or not, you ARE the CEO of your company. Regardless of whether you are still a solopreneur or you've already begun building your team, YOU are the one who has to make things happen, and steer the ship. No one else, not even the very best assistants or consultants or team can do that for you.

In the end, taking full and complete ownership for the success of your company is the most important thing you will ever do for your business. It's the moment when you stop expecting someone else to show you the path, but where you begin forging it for yourself. It's not to say you won't still get guidance along the way—I'm sure you will—but you also understand at your core that no one else is responsible for your success.

And while I've always thought of "leadership" as the ability to manage other people well, what I've come to realize is that true leadership has very little to do with effective management skills.

Instead, true leadership is the ability to shape the future through deliberate and intentional action. And while sometimes leadership involves convincing other people to follow your direction, leadership always involves being able to direct yourself.

Thus, leadership always matters, whether you are leading a team of 100 or just one. And this means that if you are alive, your leadership ability should be something that you give some serious thought to developing, at least some of the time.

And this means that to take your business—and not just your blog—to the next level, you will need to have a clear idea not only of what your brand and business is about and who you are, but also where you are heading, and where you want to go. In other words, you need to have a plan.

Creating a Plan for Your Business

A business plan sounds a little scary, but it is without a doubt one of the best things you will ever do for your blog and your business. In its most basic definition, a business plan is quite simply just a written statement of the current state of your business, your purpose and mission, a list of your business goals and objectives, the reasons you believe they are attainable, and a concrete plan for how you intend to achieve them.

Your business plan does not have to be long, nor does it have to be full of compli-cated terminology that no one understands. In fact, there might not ever be a single other person that reads it besides you. The purpose of your plan is not to impress anyone, but rather to create clarity in your own mind of where your business is now, and primarily where it is headed.

Here are a few sections you may want to include as you construct your own plan for your business.

Company Mission Statement

Your mission statement should be a succinct paragraph that sums up in 1–3 sentenc-es what your company is trying to accomplish, and what it stands for at its very core. It is something you can share with your audience and/or with your employees to let them know exactly what your business is about.

The best mission statements are generally clear, memorable, and relatively concise. For example, here is mine: I started my business as a personal lifestyle blog called *Living Well Spending Less*, which covered a wide variety of topics; including food & recipes, home & life advice, and money-saving tips. It has since grown and evolved into a full-fledged online media company called Ruth Soukup Omnimedia, that focuses on four main areas—Lifestyle, Business, Productivity, and Motivation. I've written six bestselling books, created a physical product called the Living Well Planner that we manufacture and ship all over the world, and now host a top-rated podcast called *Do It Scared with Ruth Soukup*.

And while that is a lot of different things, which gives me a pretty broad under-standing of the content marketing world, it is important to know that **my area of expertise is not all-inclusive, and it is possible that some of what I share in this book will not perfectly fit your own business or situation**. This is not a time to use flowery language or to be vague or mysterious; on the contrary, your company mission statement should unambiguously let people know what you are trying to accomplish.

Here are a few examples:

Ruth Soukup Omnimedia: We provide practical tools & the motivation to use them, to help our customers create a life they love.

Southwest Airlines: The mission of Southwest Airlines is dedication to the highest quality of Customer Service delivered with a sense of warmth, friendliness, individual pride, and Company Spirit.

TED: Spreading ideas.

Habitat for Humanity International: Seeking to put God's love into action, Habitat for Humanity brings people together to build homes, community, and hope.

Microsoft: To enable people and businesses throughout the world to realize their full potential.

Google: Google's mission is to organize the world's information and make it universally accessible and useful.

Starbucks: Our mission is to inspire and nurture the human spirit one person, one cup, and one neighborhood at a time.

Nike: Our mission is to bring inspiration and innovation to every athlete in the world.

CVS Pharmacy: We will be the easiest pharmacy retailer for customers to use.

Harley-Davidson: We fulfill dreams through the experience of motorcycling, by providing to motorcyclists and the general public an expanding line of motorcycles and branded products in selected market segments.

Core Values

Your core values are the personal beliefs that you want your business to embody and represent. These are the values that will be shared by every member of your team, and they will be represented in all that your business does. They can be one-word values, or you can create sentences to explain these beliefs in more detail. Like your mission statement, your core values should be clear, memorable, and concise.

Here are a few examples:

Ruth Soukup Omnimedia
- Get it done
- Figure it out
- Humble confidence
- Own it
- Always learn and grow

AWeber
- Foster respect and cooperation
- Listen to what people say about us
- Invite feedback
- Learn. Educate. Innovate.
- Don't take ourselves too seriously; have fun
- Create remarkable experiences

Barnes & Noble Booksellers
- Customer Service
- Quality
- Empathy
- Respect
- Integrity
- Responsibility
- Teamwork

Rackspace
- Fanatical support in all we do
- Results first; substance over flash
- Committed to greatness
- Full disclosure and transparency
- Passion for our work
- Treat fellow Rackers like friends and family

Google
- Focus on the user and all else will follow
- It's best to do one thing really, really well
- Fast is better than slow
- Democracy on the web works
- You don't need to be at your desk to need an answer
- You can make money without doing evil
- There's always more information out there
- The need for information crosses all borders
- You can be serious without a suit
- Great just isn't good enough

Target Audience

Understanding your target audience and the market you are aiming for is essential to an effective business plan. This section should include as much detailed and specific information about your blog readers or customers as possible; including age, gender, education, religious beliefs, interests, family status, income, and more. If you have multiple audiences, this should be indicated as well.

Company Assets

This is the section in which you list all of the things your business has going for it right now—all the tools in your toolbox that you can use and leverage to generate revenue and build a stronger company. Your company's top asset will most likely be your blog, but this list will also include things such as your email list, your social-media reach, and other less tangible strengths such as strong writing abilities, speaking abilities, personal expertise, a compelling story, powerful friendships, and so on.

Long-Term Business Goals

Your long-term business goals should force you to look forward to at least 2–5 years. Take a step back from the nitty-gritty, day-to-day operation of running your business and try to take a look at the bigger picture for a few moments. What is it that you are trying to accomplish in your business? How will your business make a profit? Is that profit sustainable? Are there operations you could put into place now that might make a huge difference down the road? What is your exit strategy in case you decide you don't want to do this anymore?

In addition to your big-picture strategy, your long-term business goals should also include sales and growth targets; including long-term, annual-sales goals (i.e., we want to reach $X in sales by the end of 20XX), as well as goals for the number of visitors your site receives, number of social-media followers, and number of email subscribers.

Short-Term Business Objectives

Short-term business objectives should include the main things you want to accomplish with your business in the next year. These objectives could include what products you want to create and develop, specific plans to grow your platform, or any of the other pieces you need to put in place to start working toward your long-term business goals. They should also include specific benchmarks for sales, traffic, social media, and subscribers.

Action Plan

This section of your business plan should include the specific action you plan to take to accomplish both your long-term goals and your short-term objectives. This could be a list of numbered steps that should be performed in order, or it could break down the plan month by month, into specific action items that must be done every month for the next year, along with what needs to happen in subsequent years. The more clear and specific you can be about what needs to happen when, the more able you will be able to implement your business plan in its entirety.

Build a Strong Support Team

Even with a solid business plan in place, and even if you manage to master every single time-management technique mentioned in the previous chapter, you will probably find that you still can't do it all. Blogging is essentially a black hole of endless tasks—a reality that sometimes drives my engineer-minded husband crazy. No matter how much you get done, or how efficient you are, you are never ever really finished. Depending on how large your blog is and whether you are making enough money to justify the expense, you may want to hire help.

What your helper or helpers do will depend largely on what your blog requires, what things take up most of your time, and what you simply don't want to do. Blog helpers, real-life assistants, or virtual assistants (VAs) can do everything from writing posts to managing email and social media, to negotiating with brands or managing ad space. You can also hire help to manage bookkeeping, legal issues, technical issues, and design work.

Whether or not you prefer to hire in-office help or virtual help is largely a matter of personal preference. If you work from home without a dedicated office space, having someone come to your house might not work very well, and, in some cases, may be a violation of residential code restrictions. On the other hand, it can sometimes be difficult to create a close working relationship with someone who works virtually—particularly someone who will be representing you in some sort of capacity online. Over the years I have had both virtual and in-office assistants, and I have found that I definitely prefer working with assistants face-to-face rather than virtually.

If you are thinking of hiring someone to help with your blog, whether they be virtual or live, here are a few tips that will help you find the right person for the job:

Determine what the biggest needs are for your business. Once you have created a plan for your business with clear goals and objectives, as well as an action plan for how to achieve those goals, it is much easier to see where your own deficiencies lie and where the most help is needed.

For instance, in my own business I am pretty good at big-picture strategy and creating content, but not always great about following up with details. I realized early on that I would be far more effective if I hired someone super organized and meticulous to handle all the small details I tend to let slide; such as managing my schedule, email, paperwork, and bookkeeping. It's not that I am not capable of doing those things myself, but hiring someone else to do them even better than I could, allows me to stay focused on the things I do best and keeps my business running smoothly. This, in turn, helps bring me closer to my goals!

❏ **Create a crystal-clear job description that is in line with your business objectives.** When you feel like you are drowning and desperate for help, it may seem like a waste of precious (or nonexistent) time to spend a few hours working on a job description, but this step is one of the most important things you will ever do for your business. Creating a job description forces you to evaluate exactly what kind of help you need most and what type of person would be the best fit to help you reach your goals. It also helps the person you are hiring know with certainty what the expectations of their job will be.

❏ **Ask for references or referrals.** Hiring a virtual assistant—even one whose time you buy in bulk blocks of hours—is no different than hiring any other employee. You should always conduct an interview as well as ask for references. If you're not sure where to even start looking for help, ask around to your other blogger friends, or do a Google search to see what other bloggers have written about hiring assistants.

❏ **Start with a short-term project.** Test the work ethic and skill set of your new hire by starting them with a short-term project that has a definite end. Explain that you need help with a particular project for just a few weeks. That way at the end of the project you have the chance to either walk away with no hard feelings or hire them permanently.

❏ **Create clearly defined goals and expectations.** Have a measurable list of what you want done, what the performance expectations are, as well as your timeframe for achieving your goals. Do regular performance reviews to ensure those goals are being met.

❏ **Communicate regularly.** It is hard to work with someone you can't communicate with. Check in at least several times a week to be sure you are always on the same page. This is especially important for employees who work virtually. Consider setting up a chat room on Slack, or schedule regular meetings just to check in.

❏ **Set a budget.** Know how many hours you are willing to pay per week, then keep track to make sure your assistant is making the most of the time you are paying for.

❏ **Don't be afraid to make a change.** If you don't feel that the assistant you have hired is working out for you, be willing to either talk to them about your concerns or search for someone new. Ultimately the person who works for you has to work with your style, or they will cause more stress than they alleviate.

While finding the right assistant can feel a little daunting at times, it is always worth taking the time to make sure the person you hire is a good fit for your business. A great assistant is almost always worth their weight in gold, and I have found that I have never regretted investing time, energy, and money into hiring and training the right person. On the contrary, hiring help and building a strong support team has consistently allowed me to bring my business to the next level, which ultimately pays for itself.

One Step at a Time

If you've reached the end of this book, you may be wondering how you will ever possibly complete all the tasks mentioned. How are you, as just one person, supposed to simultaneously create amazing content, drive traffic, conquer social media, monetize effectively, and create a solid business plan all at one time?

The simple answer? You can't, and you won't.

You instead will have to constantly reprioritize, reevaluate, outsource when possible, and shift your focus when necessary. In other words, you need to take it one step at a time!

My schedule looks very different now than it did ten years ago, five years ago, or even one year ago. Where I spend my time changes frequently, based on where my current focus and priorities are. I generally have three specific goals each month, which I keep track of in my Living Well Planner, and I base my schedule on the 1–3 current projects or goals I am working on. In other words, I don't try to tackle everything at once!

In the midst of a busy life and schedule, when you are just barely able to keep your head above water, the thought of actually getting ahead enough to make a plan can seem like an impossible task.

Do it anyway.

You will never regret the time you take to be purposeful about your blog and your business. If you have to, get up half an hour earlier every morning and spend that time working only on your plan and your long-term goals. Those thirty minutes a day, spread over the course of a year, will add up to a very big change.

You can do it. I know you can.

And I promise it will be worth the effort!

Chapter 12 Action Plan: Build Your Business

❏ Understand that your blog is not your business—it is an asset of your business, and that you are not a blogger, you are an entrepreneur.

❏ Create a solid plan for your business. It should include the following:
  *Company Mission Statement
  *Core Values
  *Target Audience
  *Company Assets
  *Long-Term Business Goals
  *Short-Term Business Objectives
  *Action Plan

❏ Consider hiring help in order to build a strong support team. Create job descriptions for necessary personnel, then work to find or train the right people to fill those positions.

appendix

For the most up-to-date list of our recommended resources for blogging and building your online business, please visit eliteblogacademy.com/resources.

Elite Blog Academy

Now that you've read the book, are you ready to take your online business to the next level?

Elite Blog Academy is the comprehensive online program designed to walk you step-by-step through the process of building a successful, profitable, and sustainable online business.

At EBA®, we don't just teach you how to blog, we teach you how to leverage the power of content marketing to plan, create, and grow the online business you've been dreaming of. Our proven framework get you earning more money a whole lot faster than if you tried to do it all on your own.

The doors for EBA open to the public just once a year. Don't miss your chance to get started—join our waiting list today!

You've literally got nothing to lose.

Find out more at www.EliteBlogAcademy.com

Glossary

Ad network—A company that sells Internet advertising space.

Affiliate network—A company that provides affiliate relationships for a variety of retailers.

Affiliate sales—Sales made through a special link that result in a commission.

Auto-responder campaign—Any sort of automated email or series of email that you set up to deliver value & content to your subscribers.

CPM—Cost Per Mille (Thousand).

CTA—Call to Action. A clear ask or directive, such as a call to opt in or purchase.

Deep link—An affiliate link that goes directly to a specific product or page.

Fill rate—The percentage of ads shown per page view.

Lead magnet—Also sometimes referred to as a "opt-in incentive" or "free download." Anything you give away free in exchange for an email address.

Opt in page - also referred to as a "squeeze page." This is a simple page that is set up to collect email and generally includes just one very clear CTA.

Pillar content—High quality blog posts that drive traffic.

PPC-Pay Per Click—ads that are paid based on the number of clicks they receive.

Private advertising—Advertising that is negotiated directly with the advertiser, rather than through an Ad Network.

SEO-Search Engine Optimization—the process of optimizing your web pages to result in increased search engine traffic.

Sponsored content—Blog posts or other content that is paid for or sponsored by advertisers.

The fold—A term derived from newspapers, but referring to the point at which your reader has to scroll down to see more content.

Tripwire—A product that you offer for purchase immediately after someone opts in to your list, usually for a very short time and at a significant discount.

end notes

1 According to the Bureau of Labor Statistics' Business Employment Dynamics

2 Living Well Spending Less: 12 Secrets of the Good Life by Ruth Soukup

3 Please note that there is a significant difference between WordPress.org, which allows you to create your own self-hosted blog, and WordPress.com, which is easier to set up on your own but is NOT self-hosted and will not allow you the freedom to operate or monetize your site in the way you will want to. Save yourself a lot of headaches and make sure your site is self-hosted on WordPress.org from the very beginning!

4 https://userbob.com/

5 http://blog.curalate.com/the-perfect-pinterest-pin-how-to-optimize-your-images-for-maximum-engagement-on-pinterest/

6 https://blog.hubspot.com/marketing/email-marketing-stats

CPSIA information can be obtained
at www.ICGtesting.com
Printed in the USA
LVHW021743280421
685864LV00013B/2212

9 780692 236512